Making Real Connections

Women *at* Work
Inspiring conversations, advancing together

The **HBR WOMEN AT WORK SERIES** spotlights the real challenges and opportunities women experience throughout their careers. With interviews from the popular podcast of the same name and related articles, stories, and research, these books provide inspiration and advice for taking on issues at work such as inequity, advancement, and building community. Featuring detailed discussion guides, this series will help you spark important conversations about where we're at and how to move forward.

Books in the series include:

Making Real Connections

Speak Up, Speak Out

You, the Leader

Women *at* Work

Inspiring conversations, advancing together

Making Real Connections

Harvard Business Review Press
Boston, Massachusetts

Library of Congress Cataloging-in-Publication Data

Names: Harvard Business Review Press, issuing body.
Title: Making real connections.
Other titles: Making real connections (Harvard Business Review Press) | HBR women at work series.
Description: Boston, Massachusetts : Harvard Business Review Press, [2022] | Series: HBR women at work series | Includes index.
Identifiers: LCCN 2021036003 (print) | LCCN 2021036004 (ebook) | ISBN 9781647822194 (paperback) | ISBN 9781647822200 (ebook)
Subjects: LCSH: Women—Employment. | Work—Social aspects. | Women employees—Psychology. | Interpersonal relations. | Mentoring in business. | Business networks.
Classification: LCC HD6053 .M28 2022 (print) | LCC HD6053 (ebook) | DDC 331.4—dc23
LC record available at https://lccn.loc.gov/2021036003
LC ebook record available at https://lccn.loc.gov/2021036004

ISBN: 978-1-64782-219-4
eISBN: 978-1-64782-220-0

CONTENTS

Contents

SECTION TWO

Genuine Networking

SECTION THREE
Why Sponsorship Matters

Contents

SECTION FOUR
Making Work Friendships Work

Move Beyond Small Talk and Make a Real Connection

by Emily Caulfield and Amy Gallo,
cohosts of *Women at Work*

This book, dedicated to helping you create meaningful professional relationships, is the perfect home for a coauthored introduction. We, Emily Caulfield and Amy Gallo, had worked together at *Harvard Business Review* for nearly a year before our work paths crossed as cohosts of the *Women at Work* podcast. When Emily joined the show in September of 2020, we were all in full-fledged pandemic lockdown, working from home and recording the show from our closets and bedrooms. Our first in-real-life conversation, beyond casual "hellos" in the hallway, was socially distanced at a local park when we recorded the season six trailer with the rest of the *Women at Work* team. We spread out blankets, shared cookies, and talked about how we were coping.

Emily had moved out of her studio apartment and back in with her parents. Amy was drowning in logistics of transitioning her daughter to in-person school. We discussed how unsettling it was to live with constant uncertainty and how exhausted we felt, even as we were excited to be embarking on something new. All of this turned out to be amazing fuel for candid conversations and deeper connections during an especially trying time. Of course, we don't expect all your work relationships to be born out of global crises, but this experience made something clear to us: Starting new endeavors and facing challenges can be the sparks that ignite real connections.

Starting the show was both exciting and terrifying for Emily, who had done little public speaking at work. Soon after we met, Emily sought out Amy's advice and feedback, and Amy took on an informal role as a mentor. We talked about insecurities, public speaking, and interviewing and what had gone well or fallen flat in our recording sessions. These conversations were so important to how Emily experienced her new role.

We realize now that had it not been for the show, we could easily have continued simply as work acquaintances in different departments, without an obvious reason to connect. At first glance, we may seem very different. Amy's an editor, a mom to a teenager, and a white woman who, in addition to working part-time for HBR, runs her own business as a speaker and coach. Emily's an early-career designer who recently started selling vintage clothing on the side, is a woman of color, and hasn't decided if she'll have children of her own. But it didn't take long for us to identify overlap in how we experience work and life, while also acknowledging the differences.

The relationships we've made on the show—with each other, our cohost Amy Bernstein, our producer Amanda Kersey, and others—have been one of the most meaningful aspects of our professional lives. They've allowed us to not just keep going when things got hard but to face difficulties with confidence. As we each confronted unexpected challenges at home and work, we found that trust—a key foundation we cover in the first section of this book—was an essential ingredient to bringing our full selves to our many conversations on and off the show.

For Emily, real connections at work help bridge the gap between her professional and personal identities—a way to feel more like herself in the workplace (a balancing act which can feel like a constant struggle, especially as one of the few people of color in her workplace). She thinks of her true identity as the person she is with her closest friends. Supportive colleagues, and even a true friend at work, make the workplace a safer space. Her collaboration with the women on the show has encouraged her to reach new levels of comfort with sharing her experiences and opinions. It's also given her the opportunity, with support, to experiment with and develop a new skill set, separate from her core job.

For Amy, her colleagues aren't just colleagues, but sources of support, information, and connection and an important way to stave off loneliness. It's easy for her, as an introvert, to get heads down in her work and even hide behind a screen. And when she does reach out to others, it often feels most comfortable to do that with people like herself—white working moms. Collaborating with the *Women at Work* team has been particularly meaningful for her because she's been able to work with people from different generations, racial backgrounds, and parts of the HBR organization.

While we've both found immense value in work relationships, we still have a hard time with many of the career topics covered in this collection. Amy has always dreaded networking. She feels a pit in her stomach when she thinks about walking into a room of near-strangers and having to start conversations. The process of trading business cards and small talk often feels dirty and transactional. And yet she knows that making those connections has helped—and will continue to help—her career.

Emily knows how important it is to seek out sponsorship, but admits it's incredibly challenging, especially in early career. She knows that vulnerable feeling too well—asking for help from someone who can provide a career boost but who may not see much value in a connection with her. The possibility of rejection or a work relationship with a higher up going sour is cringey, especially when you're just starting out. And when it comes to workplace friendships, she worries that they can only go so far if she's struggling to bring her most authentic self to the office.

The articles and conversations in this book have given us new tools to tackle these challenges, and we hope they will also help you as you develop the important relationships that support you as you navigate your career. Let the research-based findings, advice, and stories shared by our team, contributors, expert guests, and listeners aid you in this sometimes awkward or anxiety-ridden journey. We're sure you'll agree that the reward of genuine connections at work will be worth it.

You've probably picked up this book because, like us, whatever your gender, you want to understand the challenges women at work face, and learn how to lift up yourself and your colleagues. We've curated this collection to offer you different perspectives and different things to try. Not every piece of advice will resonate with you. Choose the counsel that stands out to you and experiment with that. Or go deep into a particular aspect of workplace relationships, whether it's networking or sponsorship, that feels daunting. We're all working on something, and we believe that this book can help you create, strengthen, or repair your important professional relationships.

Then take what we offer in this book and discuss it with the people in your life. We've found on the show that talking through these topics, our anxieties around them, the research that's been proven to work, and our own experiences helps us understand how to move forward. Offer a piece of advice or perspective you've gleaned to a friend who's starting a new role or who needs a boost before a networking event. Or talk with your peers more about why sponsorship is important for both a junior-level employee and a well-established manager. You can even use the discussion guide as a starting point.

This book is meant to inform, inspire, and make you think about how you approach relationships with colleagues. Ultimately, we hope these bonds come more easily, last longer, withstand challenges, and have a positive impact on your career.

Chances are that there are people who you casually wave hello to in the hallway or who pop up on a video call with whom you could have a stronger connection. Armed with the tools and advice in this book, now is a good a time as any for you to reach out and make those real connections. Happy reading!

Real Connections Begin with Trust

1

Sisterhood Is Trust

A conversation with Tina Opie and Beth Livingston

Emotional vulnerability makes high-quality relationships at work possible. When we've built trust and understanding with colleagues, we're more likely to be productive and engaged. Developing trusting relationships with the women we work with, particularly with those who are different from us in some way, takes care and time. But the effort is worth it—both personally and professionally. When we connect, we feel less alone in our individual struggles, and we're better equipped to push for equity.

Tina Opie, an associate professor at Babson College, and Beth Livingston, an assistant professor at the University of Iowa, are studying relationships among colleagues whose cultural identities differ by race, nationality, social class, or something else. They sat down with *Women at Work* cohosts Amy Bernstein, Amy Gallo, and Nicole Torres to talk about who was able to cultivate these high-quality relationships and what made them possible.

BETH LIVINGSTON: The idea of shared sisterhood is that we can't empower one another, we can't lift each other up if we can't be honest and show our true emotion to one another. We need to be able to say, "Hey, what you said hurt me," or "I'm dealing with this," or that we're feeling frustrated, sad, jubilant, proud, or insecure. How can we truly reach empowerment and be our full selves if we can't do that? That's what we're trying to delve deeper into in our research.

TINA OPIE: One critical takeaway of the study is that we found a high level of emotional vulnerability among women—what we call "emotional caring capacity," based on the work of Jane Dutton and colleagues at the University of Michigan.

Interestingly, Black women in particular showed lower levels of emotional vulnerability in the workplace. This tendency was even more pronounced if the work context was highly interdependent.

BETH: We found that same relationship with Hispanic women, which provided some interesting opportunities for us to talk about what we think might be going on. We wanted to avoid the mistake a lot of scholars make, in which they lump all nonwhite people together. These are very important relationships to tease out.

AMY GALLO: Can you explain the connection between emotional vulnerability and sisterhood?

TINA: If I think about the different workplaces I've been in, I often felt like I had to put on armor when I went in. While I was being as authentic as I could be, I felt that there were certain things I couldn't disclose, especially if I was bothered by something: if I was in a meeting and someone took credit for an idea; or if someone said something that I thought was offensive and there was silence in the room; or even worse, if they all laughed and I felt that it was to my detriment. You can imagine those situations: I'm upset, I'm sad, I may be angry, and what I would do is go to another floor and go into the bathroom and cry. Then I would go back downstairs and act like everything was fine.

However, there were certain people who understood. They would look at me, and we would give each other a knowing nod or wink or some kind of nonverbal signal to say, "I see you, I hear you, I'm right in this with you." After the meeting, I would get together with them, probably offsite, and have a cup of coffee and just talk about what had happened. Then these emotions would come gushing forth. That was often with other women of color, specifically Black and Latina women. But then I met Beth, and Beth is a white woman who I happen to feel especially close to around this particular topic. I think if more Black women, Asian women, Latina women, and white women had the kind of relationship that Beth and I have developed over time, the workplace would be stronger. We would be more resilient and have stronger interpersonal connections in the workplace. Our teams would be stronger, and I think the companies would be stronger, which is a competitive advantage.

BETH: That brings us to the buzzwords of "creativity" and "innovation." We hear it time and time again: How can you innovate if you don't trust people, if you're uncertain, if you're afraid you might fail? If you can't trust them, if you can't afford to be vulnerable with them, can you truly be creative and truly pursue those things that often entail risk?

So this is an opportunity for us. It's not just the right thing to do in terms of people being more comfortable and able to be themselves at work and being happier, but also in terms of how they can reach their potential professionally. Often, women—and particularly Black and Latina women—think they have to go it alone. They feel like they have to enter their workplace with a different mindset because they're well aware of the sorts of structural disadvantages that they face. What we're trying to say is that these sorts of dynamic, interpersonal relationships can help brace us for those things and help us navigate them, both for our own personal good and for our professional good.

TINA: Shared sisterhood is not just for the touchy-feely, warm and fuzzy emotions. The goal of shared sisterhood is also about empowerment, about dismantling the very structures of oppression. It's a destination, but it's also a means to an end. It's a mechanism that we're hoping can be used to improve the workplace in terms of diversity, inclusion, and equity and performance.

AMY BERNSTEIN: And engagement with all of those things. Because it's not just about crying together. It's about testing ideas against people you trust and knowing they're going to give you honest feedback and that you're there to help each other.

AMY G.: In the study, you heard directly from women who either felt emotionally vulnerable or not. I'm curious: What sort of stories did you hear, and was there anything in particular that surprised you?

TINA: One thing I found interesting was when women would try to bring up issues of equality or equity in the workplace. They were trying to be emotionally vulnerable. They might say something like, "That was really hard. That was really difficult for me." And then the white manager would respond, "Well it's difficult for everybody." The manager was overlooking the opportunity to connect more deeply. What I would advise any manager to do in that situation, but especially a white manager listening to a woman of color, is to say, "Talk to me about that. What made it difficult for you?" That's an opportunity for you to listen.

Some of the other quotes that came to my mind were when women talked about feeling isolated or that they weren't included. That took me back to some of my own experiences. In my job searches, I began to ask questions even in the interview. I was interviewing at a consulting firm—I won't say the name—and I dared to ask about what the firm was doing when people have children. The interviewer said, "Well, you're a new consultant. You shouldn't be worried about that." I didn't get that job offer, by the way. But I felt that it was incumbent on me to begin to ask those questions because at the time I was seriously dating my future husband, and we were talking about children in the future. I've always wanted to bring my whole self to work, and I felt like that was an appropriate question. Clearly, he did not.

BETH: Bringing your whole self to work is part of this idea of moving beyond just caring about the diversity to proactive inclusiveness. What was surprising to me in our findings is this sort of inclusive climate is often promoted as an unmitigated good. And we did find that across the board—the more inclusive people thought their workplaces were, the more they were able to trust their coworkers.

But what was really interesting is that as the work became more interdependent—as, "I rely on you to get my job done"—that inclusive climate wasn't enough for Black and Latina women to trust their coworkers with that sort of emotional vulnerability. Inclusion is often touted as the answer to a lot of these sorts of questions, but we're finding that it's more complicated than that. If you truly want to make people feel comfortable being themselves and bringing their whole selves—which includes not just their work-family choices but their emotions—we have to think beyond just inclusion as the answer.

TINA: That suggests that inclusion, or an inclusive climate, may be a necessary condition, but it's not a sufficient condition to get the kind of connection that we think would lead to shared sisterhood and its benefits.

NICOLE TORRES: Why is it that you can work in an inclusive environment but still not feel able to be emotionally vulnerable or bring your whole self to work with your colleagues?

TINA: An inclusive climate is operating at a macro level, while some of the examples we talked about are at the interpersonal level. There may be situations in which an organization espouses particular beliefs about diversity, equity, and inclusion, and these values may even be built into some processes. But all it takes is one or two or three interpersonal incidents that conflict with that to undermine the belief that the organization is as inclusive as we might have thought. Or we might think that "it might be inclusive for some people, but not for me."

BETH: Meanwhile, our white female respondents were very pleased with their inclusive environments. The more inclusive the environment, the more willing they were to be vulnerable with their coworkers, which is precisely as intended, I think. You would hope the more inclusivity an organization and managers build in, the more vulnerable, deep, high-quality relationships their employees would be willing to forge.

We want to avoid yet another structural solution that benefits white women to the detriment of nonwhite women. Fortunately our research is starting to be able to pinpoint where it falls apart for women of color. Some of the stories that came out were people talking about being excluded—being excluded from baby showers, from drinks after work, from conversations in the bathroom or in the hallway—and what those situations symbolized to the women in terms of how included they really were. These women of color might have felt comfortable going to their manager and talking about issues, or felt like their work was appreciated, or there were good policies and procedures in place. But when they looked around them, they still knew they were different and they still knew that they were excluded, and they weren't willing to throw a wrench into that by asking too much of co-workers that they didn't fully trust.

AMY G.: I can imagine that dissonance between "This is what my company espouses" and "This is what I personally experience" just makes the experience that much worse.

TINA: Yeah. Because it violates your expectations. And as I said, when I go into the workplace, even to this day, I still put on a little bit of armor. When an organization espouses an inclusive climate, you may put on less armor or maybe you take your helmet off, metaphorically speaking. And then when you get punched in the head by the realization that it wasn't actually true, it hurts that much more because you allowed yourself to hope.

I would love for organizations to be able to have these kinds of conversations where the woman whose manager said, "Well it's difficult for everyone," could follow up with that manager, and it would be OK for her to say, "You know, I reflected on that conversation and I really felt devalued, and I want to discuss that with you. I want to be fully committed here, and right now I'm feeling distanced from the organization and from you." It's probably naive on my part to think that that conversation could happen, but I would be hopeful that it could.

AMY G.: You're making me think. Because when I hear the word "inclusive" or "inclusive policies," I'm pretty sure it applies to me as a white woman. As a Black woman, when you hear "inclusive environment," do you question whether that includes you?

TINA: When I hear the term "inclusion," I want everyone to feel included. But it feels as though me asking for a seat at the table makes other people feel like their rights are being undermined. So "inclusion" seems to mean, "We have a language of talking about the climate and the culture, as long as it doesn't threaten people's sandboxes, as long as it doesn't make anyone feel nervous." To me, that's not really inclusion. It's just slapping on a label because it's politically correct, without fundamentally changing resources and processes to make sure it's equitable.

BETH: It becomes a signal of, "Yes, we are willing to put some degree of thought and resources behind this idea." But I think the experiences of Black and Latina women have often shown them that it's a situation of, "Trust, but verify." I'm not going to put my guard down until you show me that this is actually a safe place for me to do so. We now recognize when companies don't talk about diversity and inclusion, and that tells us something. More companies now are talking about inclusion, which is a net good. It's just not *enough* if we truly care about developing these deep, quality relationships—this shared sisterhood in which women support one another, appreciate one another, and build these deep, long-lasting relationships that can create safety for them, support for them, and also create these wonderful projects and ideas as well.

At an interpersonal level, I really love what one woman wrote when we asked our respondents to tell us a little bit more about inclusivity at their organization. She essentially said, "My group is incredibly inclusive, and we all trust each other because I'm in charge of it." This was a senior Black woman. She kept an eye out for people who seemed to be excluded and proactively nipped that in the bud. I love that quote because it demonstrates that with her being in charge, it wasn't just this idea of, "Well, it's diversity because diversity matters," although it does. Instead it's, "I had these experiences, and I know how to approach my team, my work group, to make sure that this doesn't happen again." I thought that was really a wonderful way to think about it—"We don't have any problems with this because I'm in charge."

AMY G.: What concerns me about the advice that it needs to start at the top is that so often the people who are at the top are not Black women or white women. And we reward white men in particular for being emotionally vulnerable, as well as being emotionally intelligent. Whereas when women display emotion, it's seen as weak or angry. So how do we start at the top when the playing field isn't level?

TINA: Listen, it's not level. But we're trying to create a conversation that does include white men. Tim Ryan at PwC has been doing this with diversity and inclusion and equity. He's marching right along, and he's bringing along other people. But I don't think the goal is necessarily to only start something like this in an organization that's run by a Black woman. If that were the case, I don't think it would necessarily start as quickly as we'd like, just because of the numbers.

BETH: One reason why we're really embracing this idea of shared sisterhood is because we recognize those double standards. Although we know it needs to come from the top, when we are talking about this interpersonal, dyad-level sort of interaction, our hope is that if we can start with women being emotionally vulnerable with women who are racially, ethnically, nationality-wise different from one another, then we can also start to bubble that up as well. So, I think maybe it can come from both directions.

TINA: And men can be sisters. Bernardo Ferdman, a faculty member and a consultant I love, was involved with the shared sisterhood construct when it was really in its infancy 10 or 15 years ago. I call him a sister because he has my back in an emotional way. I can call him for advice. He will do the same thing for me. We are starting with women, but the goal is to broaden out.

Adapted from "Sisterhood Is Trust," Women at Work *podcast season 3, episode 10, June 17, 2019.*

2

What Psychological Safety Looks Like in a Hybrid Workplace

by Amy Edmondson and Mark Mortensen

"Our office policy is that people should come into the office once per week. Now they are organizing a team meeting with 15 people. I guess some people seem to feel comfortable with that, but I'm not; I have a young family at home, and we have been very careful. I can't say that, though."
—Executive at a global food brand, shared privately

[To a colleague working from home] "We miss having you here with us in the office. We are seeing more people in the office these days, and it's really nice to have more people around."
—Comments made in a virtual team coffee chat

Since the Covid-19 pandemic changed the landscape of work, much attention has been given to the more visible aspects of remote work, including the challenges of managing people from a distance (including reduced trust and new power dynamics). But a far less visible factor may dramatically influence the effectiveness of hybrid workplaces. As suggested by the quotes on the preceding page, sorting out future work arrangements and attending to employees' inevitable anxieties about those arrangements will require managers to rethink and expand one of strongest proven predictors of team effectiveness: *psychological safety.*

How New Forms of Work Affect Psychological Safety

Psychological safety—the belief that one can speak up without risk of punishment or humiliation—has been well established as a critical driver of high-quality decision making, healthy group dynamics and interpersonal relationships, greater innovation, and more effective execution in organizations.[1] Simple as the concept may be to understand, Amy's work has shown how hard it is to establish and maintain psychological safety even in the most straightforward, factual, and critical contexts—for example, ensuring that operating room staff speak up to avoid a wrong-side surgery, or that a CEO is corrected before sharing inaccurate data in a public meeting (both are real-life psychological safety failure examples reported in interviews). Unfortunately, working from home (WFH) and hybrid working make psychological safety anything but straightforward.

When it comes to psychological safety, managers have traditionally focused on enabling candor and dissent with respect to work content. The problem is, as the boundary between work and life becomes increasingly blurry, managers must make staffing, scheduling, and coordination decisions that take into account employees' personal circumstances—a categorically different domain.

For one employee, the decision of when to work from home may be driven by a need to spend time with a widowed parent or to help a child struggling at school. For another, it may be influenced by undisclosed health issues (something Covid-19 brought into stark relief) or a nonwork passion, as was the case with a young professional who trained as an Olympic-level athlete on the side. It's worth noting that we've both heard from employees who feel marginalized, penalized, or excluded from this dialogue around work-life balance because they're single or have no children, often being told they're lucky they don't have to deal with those challenges. Having psychologically safe discussions around work-life balance issues is challenging because these topics are more likely to touch on deep-seated aspects of employees' identity, values, and choices. This makes such discussions both more personal and riskier from legal and ethical standpoints with respect to bias.

We Can't Just Keep Doing What We're Doing

In the past, we've approached "work" and "nonwork" discussions as separable, allowing managers to keep the latter off the table. Since the pandemic, however, many managers have found that previously off-limits topics like child care, health-risk comfort levels, or challenges faced by spouses or other family members are increasingly required for joint (manager and employee) decisions about how to structure and schedule hybrid work.

While it may be tempting to think we can reseparate the two, the shift to a higher proportion of WFH means that's neither a realistic nor a sustainable long-term solution. Organizations that don't update their approach going forward will find themselves trying to optimize extremely complicated scheduling and coordination challenges with incomplete—if not incorrect—information. Keep in mind that hybrid working arrangements present a parallel increase in managerial complexity; managers face the same workflow coordination challenges they've managed in the past, now with the added challenge of coordinating among people who can't be counted on to be present at predictable times.

Strategies for Managers

Let's start with the fact that the reasons why managers have avoided seeking personal details remain just as relevant and critical as they've always been. Sharing personal information carries real and significant risks given legal restrictions related to asking personal questions, the potential for bias, and a desire to respect employee privacy. The solution thus cannot be to demand greater disclosure of personal details. Instead, managers must create an environment that encourages employees to share aspects of their personal situations that are relevant to their work scheduling or location and/or to trust employees to make the right choices for themselves and their families, balanced against the needs of their teams. Management's responsibility is to expand the domain of which work-life issues are safe to raise. Psychological safety is needed to enable productive conversations in new, challenging (and potentially fraught) territory.

Obviously, simply saying "Just trust me" won't work. Instead, we suggest a series of five steps to create a culture of psychological safety that extends beyond the work content to include broader aspects of employees' experiences.

Step 1: Set the scene

Trite as it sounds, the first step is having a discussion with your team to help them recognize not only their challenges but yours as well. The objective of this discussion is to share ownership of the problem.

We suggest framing this as a need for the group to problem solve to develop new ways to work effectively. Clarify what's at stake. Employees must understand that getting the work done (for customers, for the mission, for their careers) matters just as much as it always has, but that it won't be done exactly as it was in the past—they'll need to play a (creative and responsible) role in that. As a group, you and your employees must come to recognize that everyone must be clear and transparent about the needs of the work and of the team and jointly own responsibility for succeeding, despite the many hurdles that lie ahead.

Step 2: Lead the way

Words are cheap, and when it comes to psychological safety, there are far too many stories of managers who demand candor of their employees—particularly around mistakes or other potentially embarrassing topics—without demonstrating it themselves or without protecting it when others do share.

The best way to show you're serious is to expose your own vulnerability by sharing your own WFH/hybrid work personal challenges and constraints. Remember, managers have to go first in taking these kinds of risks. Be vulnerable and humble about not having a clear plan and be open about how you're thinking about managing your own challenges. If you're not willing to be candid with your employees, why should you expect them to be candid with you?

Step 3: Take baby steps

Don't expect your employees to share their most personal and risky challenges right away. It takes time to build trust; and even if you have a healthy culture of psychological safety established around work, remember that this is a new domain and speaking up about buggy code is different than sharing struggles at home.

Start by making small disclosures yourself, and then make sure to welcome others' disclosures to help your employees build confidence that sharing is not penalized.

Step 4: Share positive examples

Don't assume that your employees will immediately have access to all the information you have supporting the benefits of sharing these challenges and needs.

Put your marketing hat on and market psychological safety by sharing your conviction that increased transparency is happening and is helping the team design new arrangements that serve both individual needs and organizational goals. The aim here isn't to share information that was disclosed to you privately but rather to explain that disclosure has allowed you to collaboratively come up with solutions that were better not just for the team but also for the employees. This needs to be done with tact and skill to avoid creating pressure to conform—the intent is to provide employees with the evidence they need to buy in voluntarily.

Step 5: Be a watchdog

Most people recognize that psychological safety takes time to build, but moments to destroy. The default is for people to hold back, to fail to share even their most relevant thoughts at work, if they're not sure they'll be well received. When they do take the risk of speaking up but get shot down, they—and everyone else—will be less likely to do it the next time.

As a team leader, you need to be vigilant and push back when you notice employees make seemingly innocent comments like "We want to see more of you" or "We could really use you," which may leave employees feeling they're letting their teammates down. This is a really hard thing to do and requires skill. The idea isn't to become thought police or punish those who genuinely do miss their WFH colleagues or need their help, but rather to help employees frame these remarks in a more positive and understanding way—for example, "We miss your thoughtful perspective, and understand you face constraints. Let us know if there is any way we can help." Be open about your intentions to be inclusive and helpful so that people don't see requests for their presence as a rebuke. At the same time, be ready to firmly censure those who inappropriately take advantage of shared personal information.

. . .

It's important that managers view (and discuss) these conversations as a work in progress. As with all group dynamics, they're emergent processes that develop and shift over time. This is a first step; the journey ahead comes without a road map and will have to be navigated iteratively. You may overstep and need to correct, but it's better to err on the side of trying and testing the waters than assuming topics are off limits. View this as a learning or problem-solving undertaking that may never reach a steady state. The more you maintain that perspective—rather than declaring victory and moving on—the more successful you and your team will be at developing and maintaining true, expanded psychological safety.

Adapted from content posted on hbr.org, April 19, 2021 (product #H06AWX).

3

The Three Elements of Trust

by Jack Zenger and Joseph Folkman

A s a leader or manager, you want the people in your organization to trust you. And with good reason. In our coaching with leaders, we often see that trust is a leading indicator of whether others evaluate them positively or negatively. But creating that trust or, perhaps more importantly, reestablishing it when you've lost it isn't always that straightforward.

Fortunately, by looking at data from the 360 assessments of 87,000 leaders, we were able to identify three key clusters of items that are often the foundation for trust. We looked for correlations between the trust rating and all other items in the assessment and after selecting the 15 highest correlations, we performed a factor analysis that revealed these three elements. Further analysis showed that the majority of the variability in trust ratings could be explained by these three elements.

The Three Elements of Trust

By understanding the behaviors that underlie trust, leaders are better able to elevate the level of trust that others feel toward them. Here are the three elements.

Positive relationships

Trust is in part based on the extent to which a leader is able to create positive relationships with other people and groups. To instill trust, a leader must:

- Stay in touch on the issues and concerns of others
- Balance results with concern for others
- Generate cooperation between others
- Resolve conflict with others
- Give honest feedback in a helpful way

Good judgment and expertise

Another factor in whether people trust a leader is the extent to which a leader is well informed and knowledgeable.

They must understand the technical aspects of the work as well as have a depth of experience. This means:

- They use good judgment when making decisions

- Others trust their ideas and opinions

- Others seek their opinions

- Their knowledge and expertise make an important contribution to achieving results

- They can anticipate and respond quickly to problems

Consistency

The final element of trust is the extent to which leaders walk their talk and do what they say they will do. People rate a leader high in trust if they:

- Are a role model and set a good example

- Walk the talk

- Honor commitments and keep promises

- Follow through on commitments

- Are willing to go above and beyond what needs to be done

We wanted to understand how these elements interacted to create the likelihood that people would trust a leader. We created three indices for each element, and since we had such a large data set, we experimented with how performance on each of the dimensions impacted the overall trust score. In our study, we found that if a leader scored at or above the 60th percentile on all three factors, their overall trust score was at the 80th percentile.

We compared high scores (above 60th percentile) and low scores (below the 40th percentile) to examine the impact these had on the three elements that enabled trust. Note that these levels are not extremely high or low. Basically, they are 10 percentile points above and below the norm. This is important because it means that being just above average on these skills can have a profoundly positive effect and, conversely, just being below average can destroy trust.

We also found that level of trust is highly correlated with how people rate a leader's overall leadership effectiveness. It has the strongest impact on the direct reports' and peer overall ratings. The manager's ratings and the engagement ratings were not as highly correlated, but all the differences are statistically significant.

Do You Need All Three Elements of Trust?

We were also curious to know if leaders needed to be skilled in all three elements to generate a high level of trust and whether any one element had the most significant impact on the trust rating. To gauge this, we created an experiment where we separated leaders into high and low levels on each of the three pillars and then measured the level of trust.

Intuitively, we thought that consistency would be the most important element. Saying one thing and doing another seems like it would hurt trust the most. While our

FIGURE 3-1

One element of trust is more important than the others

Relationships seem to matter more than judgment or consistency.

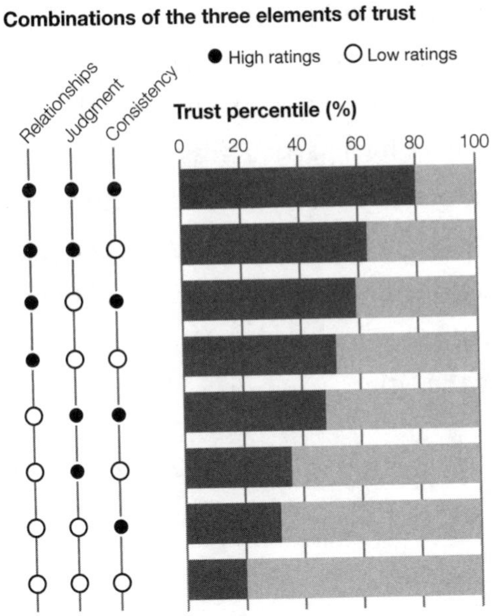

Combinations of the three elements of trust

● High ratings   ○ Low ratings

Trust percentile (%)

0   20   40   60   80   100

Relationships   Judgment   Consistency

Source: Zenger/Folkman.

analysis showed that inconsistency does have a negative impact (trust went down 17 points), it was relationships that had the most substantial impact. When relationships were low and both judgment and consistency were high, trust went down 33 points. This may be because many leaders are seen as occasionally inconsistent. We all intend to do things that don't get done, but once a relationship is damaged or if it was never formed in the first place, it's difficult for people to trust.

We often tell people that they don't need to be perfect to be an excellent leader, but when it comes to trust, all three of these elements need to be above average. Remember that in our analysis, we set the bar fairly low: at the 60th percentile. This is not a brilliant level of performance—barely above average.

We have regularly found in our research that if a leader has a preference for a particular skill, they are more likely to perform better at it. Think about which of these elements of trust you have a stronger preference for—and which you prefer least. Because you need to be above average on each, it is probably worth your time to focus on improving the latter.

Adapted from content posted on hbr.org, February 5, 2019 (product #H04RPC).

4

To Foster Trust, Organizations Need Inclusion *and* Belonging

by Michael Slepian

D iversity brings many benefits to organizations—but it is not enough on its own. An organization with a diverse workforce is not necessarily an inclusive one. Diversity efforts now often fall under the banner of "Diversity and Inclusion" for this reason, but new research shows that inclusion may also fall short because it does not necessarily lead to a sense of *belonging*.[1]

Employees may feel that they don't belong for any number of reasons, but in each case the result is the same: what researchers term an "identity threat." Defined as any situation that makes salient that one is different from others, identity threats can range from trivial to troubling. Consider the manager who talks to her low-wage employees about upcoming international travel plans, or the coworker who expresses surprise that a Black colleague doesn't conform to a stereotype. My colleague Drew Jacoby-Senghor and I set out to understand the impacts of identity-threatening situations like these that people experience on a regular basis.[2]

We recruited 1,500 individuals who spanned a range of identities, including women working in male-dominated fields, people from multiple racial groups, LGBTQ-identifying individuals, as well as people with a range of ideologies, cultures, socioeconomic backgrounds, education levels, family environments, and current hardships. The extent of diversity we examined is rare for research in the diversity space, which typically focuses on a limited set of identities, and often one at a time. Instead, we examined experiences with identity threat that transcend specific identities and contexts, allowing us to make conclusions about diversity issues in general, rather than just particular kinds of diversity.

We asked our participants whether they recently experienced identity-threatening situations, and they reported that they had many such experiences—an average of 11 in a week. When we probed further, we found that encountering identity-threatening situations was associated with feeling less included, and also reduced belonging, but importantly these were two very different experiences. We found that across a very diverse set of identities and situations, a sense of exclusion was associated with negative emotion, but feeling like one did not belong had a more pernicious effect. When employees felt like they didn't belong in the workplace, they felt that they couldn't be themselves at work. When employees feel they can't be their authentic self at work, they have lower workplace satisfaction, find less meaning in their work, and have one foot out the door.

With good reason, organizations often focus on inclusion in their diversity initiatives, but efforts toward inclusion that do not foster belonging can backfire. In a follow-up study, we asked employees about their interactions with their teammates and supervisors. In both cases, our participants made a distinction between what we call real inclusion versus surface inclusion.

When employees felt included, involved, and accepted (real inclusion), they felt like they belonged in the workplace. When employees felt like others asked for their input only because they were supposed to, or sought their opinion as someone who could represent their social group (surface inclusion), they felt like they belonged *less*. When being included for surface-level reasons, such as seeking a minority opinion, people can feel singled out on the basis of their demographics. This reduced sense of belonging works directly against inclusion efforts.

What can managers do? First, recognize but don't overemphasize differences. It is now clear that a color-blind approach does not effectively manage diversity in the workplace. Color-blind policies can leave employees feeling ignored. On the other side of the spectrum, a multicultural approach that focuses on emphasizing and celebrating people's differences can too easily slide into unintentional endorsement of stereotypes and expectancies for specific differences between groups. Organizations must strike a middle ground that allows minority members to feel included while not feeling singled out. This middle ground recognizes that people want their social groups to be included in the conversation, but they do not want to be individually included solely on the basis of their category memberships.

Second, managers should focus on the creation of identity-safe environments. Addressing underrepresentation at different leadership levels takes time, but managers today can focus on creating environments that demonstrate a value for individuals from underrepresented backgrounds and demographics. Managers should survey their employee's experiences to best understand what this should look like in their workplace and how this might be implemented (e.g., in a team-based core values exercise); but critically, the burden of this task must not be placed on minority members as this would only serve to single them out. What is acceptable behavior in the workplace? How can the organization speak to diverse audiences and consumers? Do not only look to minorities to answer these questions. Instead, include everyone in the conversation. The solution is to make *all* employees' concerns feel heard, and not single out only minority individuals or expect them to always take the lead on diversity questions.

Third, feelings of support and being valued are critical. Our study found that employees regarded organizational inclusion efforts as more surface level than real when they did not feel respected, valued, or supported by the organization. And so it is important that employees feel that support systems are available to them at the broader organizational level. Leaders must create environments where employees feel comfortable speaking up when they see something that does not seem inclusive. Formal channels should allow employees to connect with leaders and mentors, and managers would be wise to listen to recommendations from HR and employee relations representatives for best practices when it comes to reporting concerns. Employees need their concerns to feel heard rather than dismissed or diminished.

Finally, the framing of inclusion attempts influences perceptions of sincerity. When it comes to the organization as a whole, inclusion should absolutely focus on different social groups and increasing representation. But when it comes to the day-to-day, inclusion efforts should be focused more on the individual than the social group they represent. Managers should include and reach out to employees from underrepresented backgrounds, but the framing of these appeals and communications is critical. Rather than treating an employee as a representative of people like them, instead consider their unique experiences and frame requests for input along these lines. Perhaps an employee has been in a different industry, has a unique job history, or currently has a project that requires unique forms of support.

The secret to making employees feel included is getting to know the people on your team as individuals. A vestige of color-blind approaches to diversity management is a tendency to value homogeny and to seek sameness. A team with a homogenous set of viewpoints will come to a decision smoothly, but often too smoothly, overemphasizing shared perspectives and overlooking critical details or opportunities for innovation. Sameness is not an asset. Learning about individuals' unique strengths and unique experiences, and showing recognition for these, is what leads employees to feel valued and respected. This is what enables going beyond surface-level inclusion in favor of real, individual-based inclusion. Inclusion efforts may be well meaning, but without a backbone of support and respect, they may seem less than genuine.

People want their social group to be included and their individual self to belong. These are two different things. Managers can hit both targets when diversity initiatives do consider social identity, but inclusion initiatives focus on the individual. Managers should not only signal that a social identity is valued, but also that the individual is valued as a person, not just on the basis of the social group they represent. Support and recognition from coworkers, particularly those in leadership positions, foster feelings of inclusion *and* belonging.

Adapted from "Are Your D&I Efforts Helping Employees Feel Like They Belong?" on hbr.org, August 19, 2020 (product #H05T6D).

5

Repairing a Professional Relationship When Trust Has Broken Down

by Dorie Clark

I f you've spent enough time in the workforce, you almost certainly have a trail of damaged professional relationships behind you. That doesn't mean you're a bad manager or employee; it's simply a fact that some people don't get along, and when we have to rely on each other (to finish the report, to execute the campaign, to close the deal), there are bound to be crossed wires and disappointments.

When conflict happens, many of us try to disengage—to avoid the person around the office or limit our exposure to them. That's a fine strategy if your colleague is peripheral to your daily life; you may never have to work with the San Diego office again. But if it's your boss or a teammate, ignoring them is a losing strategy. Here's how to buck up and repair a professional relationship that's gone off the rails.

First, it's important to recognize that *making the effort is worthwhile.* Obviously, it'll ratchet tension down at the office if you're not glaring at your colleague every time they enter the room. But resolving this tension will actually aid your own productivity. A core tenet of efficiency expert David Allen's Getting Things Done approach is "closing open loops"—that is, eliminating unresolved matters that nag at your mind. Just as you can't rest easy until you respond to that scheduling request, you'll have a much harder time focusing professionally if you're constantly in the midst of fraught encounters.

Next, *recognize your own culpability.* It's easy to demonize your colleague (*He turned in the report late! She's always leaving work early!*). But you're almost certainly contributing to the dynamic in some way, as well. As Diana McLain Smith—author of *The Elephant in the Room*—told me in an interview, "You may be focusing on another person's downside—and then starting to behave in ways that exacerbate it." If you think your colleague is too quiet, you may be filling up the airtime in meetings, which encourages them to become even quieter. If you think they're too lax with details, you may start micromanaging them so much that they adopt a kind of "learned helplessness" and stop trying at all. To get anywhere, you have to understand your role in the situation.

Now it's time to *press reset*. If you unilaterally "decide" you're going to improve your relationship with your colleague, you're likely to be disappointed quickly. The moment they fail to respond to a positive overture or (yet again) display an irritating behavior, you may conclude that your effort was wasted. Instead, try to make them a partner in your effort. You may want to find an "excuse" for the conversation such as the start of a new project or a New Year's resolution, which gives you the opportunity to broach the subject. "Jerry," you could say, "On past projects, sometimes our perspectives and work styles have been a little different. I want to make this collaboration as productive as possible, so I'd love to brainstorm with you a little about how we can work together really well. Would that be OK with you?"

Finally, you need to *change the dynamic*. Even the best of intentions—including an agreement with your colleague to turn over a new leaf—can quickly disintegrate if you fall back into your old patterns. That's why McLain Smith stresses the importance of disrupting your relationship dynamic. In the aftermath of a conflict, she suggests actually writing down a transcript of what was said by each party, so you can begin to see patterns—where you were pushing and they were pulling. Over time, it's likely that you'll be able to better grasp the big picture of how you're relating to each other and areas where you can try something different. (If you were less vehement, perhaps they'd be less resistant.)

We often imagine that our relationships are permanent and fixed—*I don't get along with him because he's a control freak, and that's not likely to change.* But we underestimate ourselves, and each other. It's true that you can't give your colleagues a personality transplant and turn them into entirely different people; we all have natural tendencies that emerge. But clearly understanding the dynamics of the relationship—and making changes to what's not working—can lead to markedly more positive results.

Adapted from "How to Repair a Damaged Professional Relationship" on hbr.org, June 5, 2014 (product #H00UA1).

Genuine Networking

6

Networking Doesn't Have to Be a Drag

A conversation with Inga Carboni

I f you hate networking events, it may be comforting to hear that experts don't think they're a great way to build strong relationships anyway. There are more natural, less transactional, and more effective ways to make real connections with people, especially within your company.

Inga Carboni, a professor at the College of William & Mary's Mason School of Business, studies the characteristics of a strong network and common challenges women face when building theirs. She and her research partner, Rob Cross, analyzed networks within 30 organizations—about 16,000 people in total—to map who was connected to whom and how. They then interviewed hundreds of female executives about their networks. *Women at Work* cohosts Amy Bernstein and Nicole Torres spoke to Inga about her research.

NICOLE TORRES: Inga, tell us a little bit about what you found. How do you define really strong connections, and what did that look like in your research?

INGA CARBONI: One of the key aspects we found was whether these women executives had a lot of what we call "boundary-spanning relationships." These are connections with people who don't necessarily look like you, who aren't embedded in the close group of people that you spend time with in your function or your unit, or even among your friendship set. They may be in different pockets of the organization or industry.

NICOLE: So, having a lot of connections and relationships with people in lots of different areas—is that what a strong network is?

INGA: There were other aspects of strong networks that that emerged from the research, but boundary spanning is an important part. If you are connecting to those diverse pockets of the organization or the industry, you're getting slightly different perspectives on the work you're doing and the problem domains you're involved with. Exposure to different, diverse perspectives makes you more able to see a problem holistically and make better decisions. It also puts you in touch with new information. You're getting new perspectives all the time, so you're hearing new things.

The research on this goes back decades. People who have more boundary spanning in their networks get more job opportunities. They get promoted faster. They make more money. They're more likely to be involved in innovation. They're more likely to be tapped as top talent. It's a big differentiator when it comes to performance.

But we know from other research, including some of the research we did on this project, that boundary spanning poses more challenges for women than it does for men.

AMY BERNSTEIN: What are some of those challenges?

INGA: A big one was a feeling of inauthenticity. Women were saying that being proactive—reaching out and connecting with new people—felt wrong to them. They felt like they were using people.

Other research shows that when we look at why we network, it's very hard for us to think that we're doing it out of altruistic reasons, especially in the professional realm. We sometimes think, "Well, I must be very selfish, or very manipulative. . . . I just want to connect with somebody to get something from them." The problem is that if we let relationships drift and just emerge organically, we tend to hang out with people who are like us. And for women, that's a big disadvantage.

So some of the sense about networking feeling wrong is heightened for women. I suspect that has a lot to do with the pressure we put on ourselves to be relational. There was also a dislike of bothering people. I heard that from a lot of women: "I don't want to suggest we get to coffee or have a chat or have a meeting. I just don't want to bother them."

NICOLE: Did you hear any stories where women were able to overcome those fears or concerns and become better networkers?

INGA: I did talk to one woman who had seen herself passed over for a promotion and realized that she needed to change the way she was doing things. She was aware that a lot of the other women at lower levels in her organization really liked hanging out together. They would socialize with the same sort of the people and really didn't stretch too far out of their comfort zone when it came to the people that they were connecting with. She realized that she had done exactly the same thing in the earlier part of her career. It was then that she got very thoughtful and strategic about networking. She still kept a lot of those good friends, but it was being more thoughtful and strategic about building her network and how she was facilitating interactions within it that was what took her to the next level.

AMY: You've also said that women who do a good job of networking are efficient. What do you mean by that?

INGA: This is delving into some of the work of my collaborator, Rob Cross, around collaborative efficiency. We are constantly collaborating at work, and his research has uncovered that we are often on collaborative overload. Learning how to have efficiency in our interactions to make sure our network supports us and doesn't drag us down is very important. Women were much more likely to be sought out for advice than they are to seek advice, which puts them at risk for collaborative overload. A lot of people are asking them for favors, help, advice, or information. Almost every woman I interviewed, when I asked them whether there was a downside to saying no to a request for their time, said that they'd feel bad. And no man said that.

NICOLE: Can you tell us about women who were efficient collaborators? What did they do? What made them stand out?

INGA: A big part of it was how they framed collaboration. More than one woman said that they had learned that when they say yes to one thing, it means they're saying no to something else. That framework allowed them to make better decisions. So she was able to say yes when she really felt that this would be something that would align with her professional objectives and otherwise to be able to say no and to delegate it out. That was a huge differentiator.

Successful women also put a lot more structure in their day, so they weren't constantly in reactive mode. For instance, they set aside time for reflection. That's the time when you're strategizing, when you are envisioning new things, when you're managing your network and reaching out to relationships that you may have lost contact with. They were better at seeding relationships, connecting with people long in advance of actually needing them. Then, when they actually needed help, that help was there.

AMY: It sounds as if "nimbleness," another of the traits that you've noticed in successful female networkers, is connected to this idea of efficiency. Talk to us about nimbleness.

INGA: Women are more likely to form and stay in relationships with other women than men are to stay with relationships with men. Not only that, but the women's relationships get stronger and more mutual over time. Compare that to a man, who more typically will move in and out of relationships, build up new relationships, and have a lot more of what we call "network churn." Network churn is not a turnover of your core, closest, really trusted people, but of the other hundred-odd people in your life. We found that women were much more likely to keep the same people in their networks, whereas men were churning their networks—and that's what leads to nimbleness.

If you're working on projects that require you to be really agile and responsive, and you have a network that's very dynamic, you're going to be able to respond better. So the stickiness in women's relationships was preventing them from being nimble.

Now, there's a positive side to the stickiness, too: women were much better than men at building strong external networks. That's a real strength, and it opens up job opportunities for them. I know some organizations are taking advantage of this and are creating interorganizational mentorship opportunities, which has been fabulous for women. And other organizations are also leveraging this by starting up alumni networks where you're able to get your personal brand out there as an organization. You can use it as a recruitment tool. People boomerang it back and forth.

AMY: How do you respectfully deemphasize the old connections? You don't want to ghost someone, right?

INGA: It's not about rejecting the old—it's more about embracing the new. It's about being open to meeting new people and avoiding that comfortable tendency of wanting to do things with the people that you've been doing stuff with—going to the same people for advice, or going to the same sorts of lunches, or the same after-hours events.

NICOLE: Can you just talk a little bit about how energy fits into having a good, strong network? What did you see strong female networkers put out there in terms of their energy?

INGA: Rob Cross has taken a look at energizers over the last two decades. He's found that the extent to which people feel energized and excited after talking with you—like you're somebody they want to brainstorm with, somebody they want to innovate with, someone who really leaves them excited about their work—that was a four times higher predictor of a strong network than any other aspect. Being that person who pulls people toward you, who energizes other people, has a strong effect on performance. You're pulling talent toward you. You're pulling ideas toward you.

NICOLE: But how do you do that? How do you give off that kind of energy to bring people toward you with their ideas and their talent?

INGA: One of the easy aspects of it is just to exhibit positivity. We like people who are positive, who smile at us and things like that. But it turns out that men and women need slightly different things. And this might explain a finding that we had that across all these networks that we looked at, that women were more likely to be identified as energizing. But they were also more likely to be the people who were *deenergizing* others.

When we dug into this, we found two very different things. Both genders, but more so men, were saying, "I want somebody who's really knows what they're talking about, who will be able to poke holes in what I'm saying, who can pull in their expertise and show me what they're doing"—a person who we refer to as having a lot of *competence-based trust*. The fact that the person knows what they're talking about makes me excited that they're listening to me. That aspect was important to both men and women, but far more to men. What was more important to women was having a feeling that somebody cared about what they were saying. One very high-level woman, CEO of a large company, told me that she turns to her network because they say, "It's OK. You're doing good." And we need that kind of feedback. This idea of caring is called *benevolence-based trust*.

The bind comes when you're trying to be energizing to men and to women. Both of them want you to be competent, and with the women it's also very important that you be caring. You're all familiar with the trade-off between being likeable and being competent that women struggle with all the time. If they project a little too much warmth and positivity, they may be viewed as less competent. And if they don't project any warmth and positivity, then they're often identified as deenergizing. So it's a very tricky line.

The successful women were very strategic about it. They would think, "I'm going to go into an interaction, and if it's with a man, I know that I have to lead with my competence, give evidence, tell of times where they had a similar experience: 'Here's some findings that I had that might be useful to you.'" When they're interacting with women, they need to lead with warmth. They have to walk this very tricky line between being sure that they come off as caring—to avoid blowing up the gender stereotype and getting the backlash if they're not being nice enough—and also to put forward their competence. They have to make these adjustments in a way that men seem not have to have to do as much.

NICOLE: If you were going to give me advice on how to form relationships that were boundary spanning, what would you tell me to do? How would I start that?

INGA: When someone asks me that, I start by taking a look at who's already in their network. And sometimes that alone can be a shock to people when they start to realize something like, "Wow, everyone in my network is white and in their 20s and comes from the same three colleges!" I encourage people to take a look at their networks, at the similarities among people in them and where there are gaps. Where is there underrepresentation?

What are you missing in terms of age and hierarchy? As people get higher in the organization, they often miss having connections with people lower in the organization. And that's a big gap, when you're not sure what's going on for people at different parts of your organization. And when you're lower, you want to make sure that you have higher as well. You want to have vertical spanning and horizontal spanning.

Then your next step is to figure how to put yourself in a position where you'll be interacting with people who can help fill those gaps. Sometimes you'll actually know a role, or maybe even a specific person, but often you don't. I'm very against the whole "schmoozing/using" impression of networking. I encourage people to think about building authentic, real relationships. But if you're waiting for them to occur spontaneously, they're going to only occur in the places where you tend to be.

One of the most rewarding things that I did as a young faculty member was joining a faculty play group made up of tenure-track faculty who had kids under five. I would never have met people across my university in these different domains without that group. We were bonding over hanging out with our kids, and then we also got to talking about what it's like—since most of us were women—to be a woman on tenure track and being a mother. I formed some very strong relationships in there.

NICOLE: I went to a golf outing once.

INGA: Do you like golf?

NICOLE: No! But I met a lot of people outside of my usual day-to-day.

INGA: Well, sometimes people will bond over how much they hate golf when they're at those kinds of things. It drives me nuts when people tell me that they have to go this or that networking event. They know they've got to do more networking, and a networking event is better than nothing, but it's really not a great use of time. Especially if you're an introvert like me—it's torture thinking about what my elevator speech is, and working a room, and stuff like that. You're much better off taking an activity that already fits into your areas of interest, whether it's volunteering, sitting on the board of a nonprofit you are passionate about, or helping with your industry by serving on a committee. Something that puts you interacting with people. It's really not enough just to go to a conference.

Adapted from "Networking Doesn't Have to Be a Drag," Women at Work *podcast season 4, episode 2, October 21, 2019.*

7

Five Misconceptions About Networking

by Herminia Ibarra

A good network keeps you informed. Teaches you new things. Makes you more innovative. Gives you a sounding board to flesh out your ideas. Helps you get things done when you're in a hurry. And much more.

But for every person who sees the value of maintaining a far-reaching and diverse set of professional connections, many more struggle to overcome innate resistance to, if not distaste for, networking. In my 20 years of teaching about how to build and use networks more effectively, I have found that the biggest barriers people typically face are not a matter of skill but of mindset.

Listening closely to my MBA students' and executives' recurrent dilemmas, I have concluded that any one or more of five basic misconceptions can keep people from reaping networking's full benefits. Which of these are holding you back?

Misconception 1: Networking is mostly a waste of time

A lack of networking experience can lead people to question whether it's a valuable use of their time, especially when the relationships being developed are not immediately related to the task at hand. For example, Joe, a Latin American executive in a large company striving to promote greater collaboration, told me that every single coworker who visits his country asks him to meet. Last year alone he had received close to 60 people, a heavy burden on top of the day job. Rightly, he wonders whether it's the best use of his time.

But just because networks can do all these things, it doesn't mean that yours will. It all depends on what kind of network you have and how you go about building it. Most people are not intentional when it comes to their networks. Like Joe, they respond to requests, but reach out to others only when they have specific needs. Reaching out to people that you have identified as strategically important to your agenda is more likely to pay off.

Misconception 2: People are either naturally gifted at networking or they are not, and it's generally difficult to change that

Many people believe that networking comes easily for the extroverted and runs counter to a shy person's intrinsic nature. If they see themselves as lacking that innate talent, they don't invest because they don't believe effort will get them very far.

Stanford psychologist Carol Dweck has shown that people's basic beliefs about "nature versus nurture" when it comes to personal attributes like intelligence or leadership skill have important consequences for the amount of effort they will put into learning something that does not come naturally to them. People with "fixed" theories believe that capacities are essentially inborn; people with growth mindsets believe they can be developed over time.

As shown in a paper by Kuwabara, Hildebrand, and Zou, if you believe that networking is a skill you can develop, you are more likely to be motivated to improve it, work harder at it, and get better returns for it than someone with a fixed mindset.[1]

Misconception 3: Relationships should form naturally

One of the biggest misconceptions that people have about networking is that relationships should form and grow spontaneously among people who naturally like each other. Working at it strategically and methodically, they believe, is instrumental—somehow even unethical.

The problem with this way of thinking is that it produces networks that are neither useful to you nor useful to your contacts because they are too homogenous. Decades of research in social psychology shows that left to our own devices, we form and maintain relationships with people just like us and with people who are convenient to get to know to because we bump into them often (and if we bump into them often, they are more likely to be like us).

These "narcissistic and lazy" networks can never give us the breadth and diversity of inputs we need to understand the world around us, to make good decisions, and to get people who are different from us on board with our ideas. That's why we should develop our professional networks deliberately, as part of an intentional and concerted effort to identify and cultivate relationships with relevant parties.

Misconception 4: Networks are inherently self-serving or selfish

Many people who fail to engage in networking justify their choice as a matter of personal values. They find networking "insincere" or "manipulative"—a way of obtaining unfair advantage and, therefore, a violation of the principle of meritocracy. Others, however, see networking in terms of reciprocity and giving back as much as one gets.

One study discovered that views about the ethics of networking tend to split by level.[2] While junior professionals were prone to feeling "dirty" about the instrumental networking they knew they had to do to advance their careers, their seniors did not feel the slightest bit conflicted about it because they believed they had something of comparable value to offer.

The difference came down to confidence or doubt about the worth of their contributions, with junior professionals feeling more like supplicants than parties to equitable exchange. My own research suggests that the only way to conceive of networking in nobler, more appealing ways is to do it and experience its value, not only for you but for your team and organization.[3]

Misconception 5: Our strong ties are the most valuable

Another misconception that gets in the way of building a more useful network is the intuitive idea that the most important relationships in our network are our strong ties—close, high-trust relationships with people who know us well—our inner circle. While these are indeed important, we tend to underestimate the importance of our "weak ties"—our relationships with people we don't know well yet or we don't see very often—the outer circle of our network.

The problem with our trusted advisers and our circle of usual suspects is not that they don't want to help. It's that they are likely to have the same information and perspective that we do. Lots of research shows that innovation and strategic insight flow through weaker ties, which add connectivity to our networks by allowing us to reach out to people we don't currently know through the people we do.[4] That's how we learn new things and access far-flung information and resources.

. . .

One of the biggest complaints that the executives I teach have about their current networks is that they are more an accident of the past than a source of support for the future. Weak ties, the people on the periphery of our current networks and those we don't know very well yet hold the key to our network's evolution. Our mindsets about networking affect the time and effort we put into it and, ultimately, the return we get on our investment. Why widen your circle of acquaintances speculatively, when there is hardly enough time for the real work? If you think you're never going to be good at it? Or, that it is in the end, a little sleazy, at best political?

Mindsets can change and do but only with direct experience. The only way you will come to understand that networking is one of the most important resources for your job and career is try it—and discover the value for yourself.

Adapted from content posted on hbr.org, April 18, 2016 (product #H02TMD).

8

Remote Networking as a Person of Color

by Laura Morgan Roberts and Anthony J. Mayo

In remote work situations, where people cannot rely on impromptu elevator conversations or watercooler chats with coworkers, it can be tempting to turn inward, but in fact, the need for networking is even *more* important. During challenging economic times, both external and internal networking can provide energizing social connections, firm and industry insight, personal affirmation, social support, and access to career opportunities. In particular, our interactions with people whose backgrounds and perspectives differ from our own helps us to become smarter, more creative, and better equipped to solve difficult problems.

Building relationships across difference does not come naturally or automatically, however. According to our research, networking can be especially challenging for professionals of color, who may not only experience general discomfort, but also face unique challenges in not being perceived as powerful, credible, or resourceful. This deficit-based assessment often results in less outreach and relationship-building. Professionals of color are also at higher risk of becoming isolated, struggling to navigate the racial boundaries at social events; in particular, they hesitate to share information about themselves, which limits their ability to be authentic at work and to build deep relationships.

The common mantra about working "twice as hard to get half as much" unfortunately rings true in economic data, which suggests that Black men and women must outwork and outperform their white counterparts to be seen as comparably skilled.[1] Our research shows that this extends to activities like networking, where workers who differ from their counterparts report feeling excluded and marginalized, which makes it harder for them to believe that their social capital is valued.

At the same time, the world of work in the aftermath of the pandemic may offer opportunities for professionals of color to network in ways that are more comfortable and authentic. By identifying these strategies, professionals of color can build new relationships that can elevate their careers over the short and long term. One big hurdle to capitalizing on these possibilities, however, is confronting the ways in which internal and external networking is perceived by professionals of color.

How Professionals of Color Perceive Networking

Before the emergence of Covid-19, and in collaboration with The Partnership, Inc., we surveyed 300 mid- to senior-level professionals of color in the United States about their perceptions of networking and how frequently they engaged in it. More than half reported that they were "too busy" to participate in networking events, 30% cited work-related conflicts, 17% reported they preferred to focus on work, and 17% associated networking with "playing politics."

One professional stated, "My personal cost/benefit analysis suggests that networking events do not reap as much benefit as other professional and personal activities." A Black executive in the financial services sector noted, "I definitely am not a natural networker per se. My relationship building has primarily been through the lens of my work and using that as the basis to build relationships. I'm not comfortable with inorganic interaction. I'm not the 'Let's go to a cocktail reception and strike up a conversation' type of person."

Broadly, networking was not a top priority for the majority of professionals in our study; fewer than half felt it was essential for their careers, and senior executives were even less likely to consider networking essential, compared with early-career professionals. (Compare this with a 2017 global LinkedIn survey, where 80% of professionals said networking was important for career success—though, interestingly, half of respondents said they were too busy to network, which is similar to our findings.[2]) This head-down attitude results in a startling statistic: 82% participated in networking activities less than once per month.

This lack of networking clearly has a cost, one that is often larger for marginalized individuals in the organization. Ultimately, this low frequency is not nearly enough for people who are serious about investing in the high-quality connections that are essential for well-being and career success.

As a Black venture capitalist stated, "We're just too heads down on our work, and we're not doing the networking, which is hurting us. We're not spending the time to build rapport with the people who are making the decisions about who gets the next job, who gets the next big opportunity. They don't know us. They don't have a rapport with us. They haven't heard us talk about what we've accomplished. Then we're not going to come up in the conversation when they decide who's going to get the next high-level job."

Changing the Paradigm: How Professionals of Color Can Leverage Remote Networking

Despite these findings, our research also revealed several networking activities that professionals of color are likely to engage in (see table 8-1).

In fact, the Covid-19 crisis may have created new, more attractive opportunities for building relationships with people who can share valuable information about opportunities, provide honest assessments of strengths and weaknesses, and advocate for promotions.

First, many of the obstacles that our study participants identified can be removed in this time of physical distancing. For example, several reported that the event locations were often too inconvenient for travel, or that

TABLE 8-1

The forms of networking professionals of color prefer

Professional conferences	73%
Community volunteering	58
Social media	52
Taking initiative to meet new people	51
Employee resource groups	45
Special committees or task forces	45
Nonprofit boards	42

Source: Survey of 300 mid- to senior-level professionals of color in the United States, February–March 2018.

designated "networking opportunities" conflicted with other work obligations. Other barriers included the cost of events. When in-person professional conferences went on hold, less expensive virtual events, community volunteering, and social media interactions stepped in and continue to this day.

Here are some other ways in which professionals of color can leverage networking strategies to stay connected and visible while working remotely, though these actions would likely benefit anyone in the current work arrangement.

1. Reactivate dormant connections

Reach out through social media or direct message to individuals you've known for a while but haven't connected with in some time. When everyone is busy coming and going, these relationships can fall off the radar. But they are especially valuable in helping you to feel more connected and authentic during crises, reminding you of your core values, goals, and dreams. They may also be aware of new job opportunities, which can be valuable information as companies shift to meet new economic pressures.

2. Participate in learning communities

When we asked our respondents about how they most commonly networked, the top response was participating in professional conferences, most of which were canceled or postponed during the pandemic. But a host of virtual learning opportunities have launched in their place, providing opportunities to meet new people through workshops and discussion groups. Most colleges and universities are offering a variety of virtual seminars and other learning opportunities that support education and community building. Social media channels also offer interest-based groups where people can share resources and suggestions for dealing with work-related challenges.

3. Maintain periodic outreach to champions and sponsors

A common thread in the success stories of professionals of color is the support of a champion or sponsor—someone in the organization that not only provides advice but helps to create the conditions for new opportunities and increased visibility. It is critical to sustain these connections, especially in light of greater uncertainty in the economic landscape.

4. Network through community service

Our survey showed that people are more enthusiastic about networking opportunities that are coupled with organized outreach events. Through these activities, they are more likely to meet people with common intellectual, business, and/or values-based interests. For professionals of color in our studies, these community service activities often include targeted outreach toward underserved and marginalized communities, such as mentoring youth of color and serving on not-for-profit boards. Community-based networking events are attractive because they tap into a sense of collective identity and higher purpose. They also help to counteract the belief that networking is motivated purely by self-interest.

5. Focus on shared networks and organize group networking

We also discovered, through follow-up interviews and case studies of Black executives, that those most likely to invest in networking were able to reframe their perceptions of these activities from self-focused to other-focused. Conversations about networking became livelier when professionals talked about networks to which they *belonged*, rather than networks that they *possessed*. A discussion of "my" network can be off-putting, casting one as an instrumentally focused power broker who may put personal advancement ahead of relationship strength. Conversely, practices that build shared networks (e.g., "our" alumni/community group/professional association networks) were evident in examples of people who were willing to make time in their busy schedule to field phone calls from strangers, answer informational questions from acquaintances, and help position other people for personal and professional success. As one professional of color stated, "Networking is essential to the soul. It is not about me."

Black alumni associations are useful exemplars of shared networks, which meet regularly in regional groups, facilitate formal service and fundraising events, and also function as an insider channel for looping people typically in the margins into promising developmental opportunities. These unique forms of shared networks also provide rich contexts of cultural familiarity, which helps workers and their families to create a sense of community in companies and cities where they may be demographically underrepresented. For instance, one Black executive said, "We can speak in shorthand to one another and say, 'How are you going to deal with this issue?' 'We're all trying to accomplish similar things....' There's an inspirational level to it."

6. Participate in remote employee resource groups

The value of employee resource groups (ERGs) has been called into question recently, under the rationale that they fail to promote inclusion.[3] However, our findings suggest that ERGs provide an important vehicle for building and sustaining relationships—an especially challenging task for professionals of color—which should be systematically supported for the benefit of both employees and their companies. Now more than ever, firms should invest in initiatives that support the strategic aims of ERGs to build community and strengthen business leadership.

It must be stated that the burden of contact should not be borne solely by professionals of color. A lack of physical presence can exacerbate the "invisibility conundrum" that many of these professionals experience as being one of very few people like them in their organizations or fields—that is, their anomaly status often makes it more difficult to be part of key decisions and their "otherness" can make them invisible. Moving to a virtual environment can make matters worse, as it becomes far easier for connections to fracture, even inadvertently. That is why it is so important for professionals of color to ensure regular contact and interaction with their managers and peers—and why managers and other industry leaders must proactively stay in contact with their colleagues of color as well.

For professionals of color who struggle to be seen and heard, it is critical to sustain and cultivate connections inside and outside of work. The strategies that we have outlined in this article are especially important for people of color today, but they are also actions that can apply to anyone who seeks a more proactive role in managing their career.

Adapted from content posted on hbr.org, September 7, 2020 (product #H05U02).

9

Do Women's Networking Events Move the Needle on Equality?

by Shawn Achor

few years ago, I was flying home from the Conference for Women, where I had been invited to speak. I was carefully holding a copy of the conference program on my lap—my mom likes to save them, and I wanted to be a good son and bring her back an unwrinkled copy. The guy sitting next to me on the airplane noticed it and asked me about the conference. I told him it's a series of nonprofits across the country that run conferences for women from all industries to talk about leadership, fairness, and success. He then surprised me by saying, "I'm all for equality, but I'm not sure what good a conference will do." Done with the conversation, he put on his headphones, content in his cynicism as I stewed, trying to come up with the best, albeit incredibly delayed, response.

By the time I landed, I realized the best response to such a cynical attitude would be data. It won't change anyone's mindset to just claim that connecting women is "important" and will "have an impact at work and in society." We need to show that it actually does. That's why Michelle Gielan, bestselling author of *Broadcasting Happiness*, and I partnered with the Conference for Women to see if we could test the *long-term effects* of uniting women. Spoiler alert: The results astounded even us.

In our initial study of 2,600 working women across functions and industries attending Conferences for Women in several U.S. states, we examined a number of outcomes that occurred in the year after they attended. Since women who attend a conference might be different demographically and psychographically from women who elect not to, we used a control group that was made up of women who had signed up for a conference but had not yet attended.

As part of the study, we were looking for two types of positive outcomes for women who attended a conference: financial (pay raises and promotions) and intellectual (increased optimism, lower stress levels, and a feeling of connection). Since we were looking at financial outcomes, we made sure the time period we studied was the same for the research group and the control group to account for any changes in the larger economic landscape.

For the women who'd signed up for the conference but had yet to attend, 18% received a promotion during the time period we studied, compared with 42% of women who had already attended the conference. In other words, in the year after connecting with peers at the Conference for Women, the likelihood of receiving a promotion doubled. (I wish I could find that guy on the plane to share this stat with him.)

In addition, 5% of the women in the control group received a pay increase of more than 10%, compared with the 15% of women who had attended the conference. That means that in one year, attendees had triple the likelihood of a 10%+ pay increase. (Remember, this isn't selection bias—women in the control group were also signed up to attend a future conference.)

We also polled the women who'd attended the conference about how it affected their overall outlook. Seventy-eight percent of them reported feeling "more optimistic about the future" after attending. While we could not compare this with the control group's outlook, this still seemed like a significant finding to us, in part because of what we know about how a positive mindset can affect other aspects of life. In my HBR article "Positive Intelligence," I describe how optimism can create a "happiness advantage," where nearly every business and educational outcome improves as a result.

Perhaps most tellingly, 71% of the attendees said that they "feel more connected to others" after attending. This is important. In my book *Big Potential*, I outline why the greatest predictor of success and happiness is social connection. Research has shown that social connection can be as predictive of how long you will live as obesity, high blood pressure, or smoking.[1] There is power in connection. I start *Big Potential* with the story of a study of synchronous lightning bugs from Indonesia, in which researchers at MIT found that if lightning bugs light up alone, their success rate for reproduction is 3%. If they light up simultaneously with thousands of other lightning bugs, their success rate rises to 86%. By lighting together, they could space themselves out to maximize resources, and the increase in their collective brightness would help them be seen for up to five miles! I wrote *Big Potential* because I have found that if people feel as though they are trying to get out of depression alone, or fighting inequality alone, or striving for success alone, they burn out and the world feels like a huge burden. But there is a powerful, viable alternative to individually pursuing success and happiness: *doing it together.*

I'm not sure *every* conference would have such a long-term positive impact. I have been to quite a few where either the conference is not engaging or the attendees are disengaged and on their phones. I think it's safe to say there is an inverse relationship between the benefits you'll get from a conference and the time you spend on your laptop or phone.

The keys to a beneficial conference, based on my experience speaking at more than 900 conferences over the past 12 years, are (1) a sense of social connection felt by the attendees, (2) engaging sessions, (3) leaders who role model and exemplify the qualities that the conference is attempting to instill, (4) a memorable moment, and (5) a realistic assessment of the present with an optimistic look to the future. Based on the responses of the women in this sample group, we see elevated optimism and social connection, as well as superstar role models (for example, Michelle Obama and Brené Brown also spoke at the event I went to). Moreover, many of the sessions offered practical applications for moving forward at work, such as how to ask for a raise, or stories from other women to let attendees know that their experiences at work are not unusual or isolated.

Laurie Dalton White, founder of the Conferences for Women, adds, "Something special happens when you see that you are not alone. Making connections and building relationships with other attendees and speakers helps women form an understanding of their worth, and then they learn strategies to ask for promotions, seek fair pay, and even become mentors to others. We invite women like Michelle Obama and Sheryl Sandberg to speak at our conferences not just because of their own personal success stories, but because they are role models who inspire women in both big and small ways."

There is power in connecting, and it's not just about gender. Men and women alike can benefit from the power of connection. If you are a manager, encourage your employees to go to events where they can connect with others to remind them that they are not pursuing success and happiness alone. If you are a CEO, invest in conferences that help build up all members of your organization, regardless of where they sit in the organizational hierarchy.

We have so much more to learn about the value of connection in a hypercompetitive world. To the guy sitting on the plane: This research shows that cynicism regarding women's conferences and initiatives is unfounded, unconstructive, and uninformed. To the rest of us seeking a positive path forward at work and in society, regardless of gender: We must pursue happiness and success together. Like the lightning bugs, rather than trying to light up the darkness alone and in isolation, there is power when we add our light to something bigger. In doing so, we shine brighter.

Adapted from content posted on hbr.org, February 13, 2018 (product #H045O0).

10

How to Protect Your Time Without Alienating Your Network

by Dorie Clark

I t's a law of nature: The further you rise, the more people will make demands on your time. Some of those requests are self-interested: the informational interview, the job advice, the request for a connection, a recommendation letter, or angel funding. Others may be quite beneficial to you: the offer of a paid speaking engagement or a prestigious media interview opportunity or an invitation to an exclusive conference. The easy answer is to ignore all of these requests, deleting them as they come in—or even more extreme, to declare some form of email bankruptcy. But of course, that risks alienating some of your biggest advocates.

I feel genuine empathy for one top business thinker with whom I had a heart-to-heart at a conference a couple of years ago. She was overwhelmed and miserable with the amount of correspondence she received; it literally pained her. Her answer? She pretty much ignored everything, including my follow-up requests to interview her for a (very well-read) publication and, later, to endorse my forthcoming book. I know she's busy and I like her a lot, but total silence is not the mark of a friend, or even a passing-grade acquaintance. So how can you protect your time—and accomplish your more pressing priorities—without being a jerk to allies? Here are three strategies.

Scale your time

I'm fortunate that there are plenty of people who'd like to connect with me for meals or drinks or coffee: It's a good problem to have. The downside, of course, is that I don't have time for every request. Yesterday, I received an email from a Wharton School student who had attended a guest lecture I'd given there 18 months ago. Very politely, he thanked me for my talk, shared how he'd been implementing my suggestions, and then asked if I could "spend 20–30 minutes on the phone for a few points" on how he might best take advantage of a new opportunity. He sounds terrific and I'd like to help, but it's just not feasible to do this for every student who requests it. Instead, I'm going to follow a tip that tech opinion leader Robert Scoble shared with me when I interviewed him for my book *Stand Out*. Instead of responding to emails one at a time, Scoble asks his interlocutors to post their questions on Quora so that others can see and benefit from his responses. I won't use Quora, but I'll ask the student to email me his question. I'll respond electronically and will later turn it into a blog post. Similarly, instead of one-on-one coffees, I'll often organize dinners to bring together interesting groups of people who could also benefit from knowing one another.

Don't overestimate your own importance

I'd been convening a series of such dinners in New York City for a number of months, bringing together authors to meet each other, make connections, talk about book marketing, and the like. When I realized a mutual friend knew one thinker I admired, I asked her to make an introduction and invited him to our next gathering. In the past, I'd had prominent authors jump at the chance, excited to spend a night trading ideas with like-minded colleagues. But this potential guest was more skeptical. "I might have a conflict that night," he wrote. "But can you let me know who's going to be there and I'll see if I can get around to it?" In other words: Was there anyone important enough to be worth his time? I humored him with the list, and he agreed to attend—until the event was threatened by inclement weather. He wrote back eagerly: *Is the event still on? Who's still coming?* Demanding a guest list is the equivalent of craning your neck at a cocktail party to see if someone more worthy of your attention has walked in the door. Of course, it's important to guard your time and be selective about which events you attend, but there has to be a baseline of trust and humility, especially when you've been introduced by a mutual contact. Make your best decision about whether to attend—and stick to it.

Make a choice about what to be bad at

Last year, I'd reached a point where I was feeling overwhelmed about my contacts. I knew I should be keeping in touch with people, but the volume had gotten so great, I didn't know where to start. I signed up for a service called Contactually that helps track your interactions and sends you reminders when you've been out of touch with key people too long. A few weeks ago, they offered a free analysis of my email performance over the past year, looking for patterns and weak spots. Desperate for illumination, I had them run one . . . and got a D+, by far the worst grade I've ever received for anything besides handwriting. It was sad, true, and quantified before my eyes: I'm very pokey at responding to most emails. But I do have a policy: Unless it's a spammy message, I *will* respond eventually. It's not perfect, but it's a trade-off I feel comfortable making thanks to Frances Frei and Anne Morriss's excellent book *Uncommon Service*, in which they argue that in order to become truly great at something (such as a bank being open long hours), companies have to make an equally important choice about something to be bad at (such as offering unusually low interest rates on deposits). The same advice works for individuals. I've chosen to be bad at email response time because it's less important to me than serving clients or creating new content. But I'll never let it get to the point where there's *no* response. (My hero in this regard is Wharton professor Adam Grant, who hired an assistant just to help him respond to each and every message he got as the result of a popular *New York Times Magazine* profile. Though I make some use of virtual assistants, I'm now contemplating hiring someone full time.)

. . .

Managing your time is a constant balance—too loose, and you spin off in a million unproductive directions; too tight, and you eliminate serendipity and come off like a controlling prima donna. We all have to find the procedures that work for our lives and schedules, but it's important to do it in a way that doesn't needlessly alienate others.

Adapted from content posted on hbr.org, February 6, 2015 (product #H01V9I).

11

How to Maintain Your Professional Network over the Years

by Rebecca Knight

Everyone knows it's important to build a network. But once you've made a connection with someone, how do you maintain it over the long haul so that you can call the person when you need help (e.g., a job reference or a professional favor)? How frequently should you be in touch with your contacts? And how do you balance efforts to bring in new people while staying in touch with those you've known for a while?

What the Experts Say

Networking is linked to many measures of professional success—including getting promoted, having influence, earning more money, and feeling more satisfied in your career. "Research shows that networks give people access to information, such as advice and problem-solving assistance, among other benefits," explains Francesca Gino, a professor at Harvard Business School and coauthor of the HBR article "Learn to Love Networking." "Over time, this information access helps people acquire the knowledge and competencies that are necessary to succeed at work and better handle challenges." Your network not only helps you thrive in your current job; it also helps you uncover your next one, according to Dorie Clark, the author of *Reinventing You*. "For most professionals, the job offers they receive and consulting offers they land are a direct result of their network," she says. "If you're not staying in touch with people from your past, you're cutting off a lot of potential opportunities." Here are some strategies for maintaining those ties.

Prioritize

First "make a clear-eyed determination about who in your network you want to prioritize," says Clark. She suggests "grouping your contacts into buckets" of categories—for example, current clients, potential clients, influential and powerful colleagues, and "friends who are real connectors"—and then figuring how best to allocate your attention. But priorities aren't always clear-cut, warns Gino. There may be people you keep in touch with for no other reason than you enjoy their company or you have similar interests. "Think about the ways in which your relationships make [you] better off. If you're a happier person when you talk to a particular friend or colleague, make a point to do so on a regular basis," she says.

Show you care

Next, Clark recommends thinking about the "different tools in your arsenal to stay in touch"—email, phone calls, coffee dates, social gatherings, and handwritten notes—and how you can best use these to nurture your relationships. The key to maintaining a professional network, she says, is to "be in the orbit" of the people you're trying to cultivate so that, if you require their assistance down the road, "you are still top of mind." The best way to do this is to "take steps that demonstrate you care about the other person and that you're interested in his or her life," she adds. "Be aware of when news or information triggers you to think of that person." Perhaps you read a book a former colleague might like, attended a lecture about a subject she's interested in, or recently met a connection of hers. "That's a good time to get in touch." Adds Gino, "Good relationships need to be nurtured. If you care for that person to be in your network, you should avoid contacting him or her only in a moment of need."

Be strategic with social media

In the Information Age, you can easily stay connected to people from your past for digital eternity but, cautions Gino, an overreliance on social media to maintain your professional network can be dangerous. "Just as a phone call is not the same as conversing in person, social media has a different level of fidelity," she says. "Sometimes social media tricks us into believing we have a strong connection with someone when, in fact, that connection only exists in that single plane of existence." Still, adds Clark, you can use social media to your advantage. You might, for instance, trade direct messages with your contacts on Twitter, repost content they've created on LinkedIn, or retweet blogs and articles they've highlighted. Even better, "take the conversation off-line," she says. "If you notice that your friend was just promoted or had some other success, celebrate her win by giving her a call or sending her a note."

Offer to help

Another way to remain in good standing with your contacts is to "look for ways you can be helpful to them," says Clark. "Listen carefully" to what they say and the challenges they face. "Perhaps your contact is struggling to help his son find an internship, and you know that your firm has them. Offer to make a connection. Perhaps your former colleague tells you she's interested in starting to do more video at her job, and you just read a book on the subject. Send it as a gift." Make sure your motives are pure, however. "Helping others is a fine thing to do, but doing so in order to gain favor only serves to demonstrate to those you intend to impress that you are shallow—the opposite of your goal," says Gino. "Being genuine and authentic and sincere is much more likely to create a sense of respect."

Don't brag

Although it's good for your network to know about your professional successes and promotions, you don't want to gain a reputation as a braggart. Gino recommends a milder form of self-promotion: simply "informing the other person about what you have been up to in a way that provides information he or she does not have." Clark concurs. "You don't need to bang the drum," she says. "If you have had positive relationship with someone in the past and you're confident she thinks you are a good person, you don't need to go on a long-standing promotional campaign. Just stay in touch and express interest in her life. That'll keep a positive memory alive."

Don't force friendships

If there is someone from your past that "you want to keep up with, and you've tried multiple times but the other person just doesn't seem to have that same desire," it's probably a sign to give up, says Clark. "Maybe he's just really busy or his spam filter is particularly aggressive," but it's also likely he's not interested in staying connected. Gino agrees. "Don't become overly concerned with connections that aren't mutual because, just as with other relationships, seeming desperate only makes you less desirable," she says. She suggests trying to become friends with the person's friends instead. "Play the long game but always be genuine," she says. "Shallow connections are not worth the effort and can fade quickly."

Regroup from time to time

Clark recommends doing an "audit" of your professional ties every six months or so. "You need to look at your list of contacts and ask, Is it still accurate? Who should I add? Who is no longer quite as relevant?" Over time, Clark says, "you will cycle people" in and out of your network. This doesn't mean you won't talk to [old contacts], of course; it's just not going to be as often. Bringing new people into your circle and staying in touch with long-time contacts "shouldn't feel like a balancing act at all if you're doing it well," says Gino. "Continuously mix old and new when possible"—that is, introduce people you've just met to others in your network, which gives you an opportunity to learn more about both of them. "This opens up relationships that may have stagnated," she adds.

Principles to Remember

DO:

- Decide who you want to stay in touch with and how often you want to reach out

- Make use of all the communication tools in your arsenal, including email, phone, coffee dates, social gatherings, and handwritten notes

- Look for ways you can help your contacts with the professional and personal challenges they face

DON'T:

- Go overboard on social media; be strategic about how you use it

- Brag about your accomplishments

- Kill yourself trying to network with everyone you've ever met; keep a running list of relevant contacts and audit it from time to time

Adapted from content posted on hbr.org, September 20, 2016 (product #H0352X).

Why Sponsorship Matters

12

Sponsorship: Defining the Relationship

A conversation with Rosalind Chow

To get ahead at work, we need support from people besides our boss. Sometimes that comes in the form of mentorship, where a person with more experience gives us advice or guidance on how we can improve. But there is another kind of support that is equally if not more important: *sponsorship*, where someone with a lot of power in the company advocates on our behalf.

Having a sponsor—someone who can use their influence to push your career forward—is invaluable. But how exactly sponsors do this, and what your role is in making it happen, isn't always clear-cut. Who should we be seeking to sponsor us? Should sponsors be candid with their protégés about what they're doing on their behalf?

Women at Work cohosts Amy Bernstein, Amy Gallo, and Nicole Torres posed these questions and others to Rosalind

Chow, an associate professor at Carnegie Mellon University's Tepper School of Business who studies sponsorship. She helped clarify some of the ambiguity and discussed what should be transparent and what should stay unspoken.

NICOLE TORRES: To start with, could you help us understand the distinction between mentorship and sponsorship?

ROSALIND CHOW: Mentorship is about changing the mentee. It's about developing either the skill set of the person who's being mentored or giving them advice. Sponsorship, on the other hand, doesn't necessarily have to engage the protégé physically in the moment at all. Someone could get sponsorship without knowing. It's a purely external form of support that a sponsor can provide. It's not about changing how the protégé thinks about themselves; it's about changing how other people perceive the protégé and creating situations where they have opportunities to shine.

NICOLE: I love that distinction.

ROSALIND: Another kind of important distinction I would make between mentorship and sponsorship is that mentorship is more about the provision of time. Being a mentor means putting a lot of time into someone—one-on-one meetings where you're listening to them or giving them advice on how they ought to proceed in a tricky situation. But sponsorship is really about the provision of social capital.

For instance, if you invite someone to a conference that they would never otherwise have gone to, you may not yourself go to that conference, but you have provided this incredible opportunity that they wouldn't otherwise have had access to. That's not really you making extra effort or spending time. But it is in a way about putting your reputation on the line in a way that mentorship doesn't necessarily require. Another way to think about it is, "If this person succeeds, does it impact my reputation?" With mentorship, it's not clear that if the mentee succeeds or doesn't succeed, that the mentor is actually going to be impacted. With sponsorship, if the protégé does really well, that reflects well on the sponsor; but if the protégé fails, that has negative ramifications. So the interconnection of the reputation becomes intertwined in a way that I don't think is true of just pure mentorship.

AMY BERNSTEIN: We've heard of situations where protégés never actually ask to be sponsored. Is that typical?

ROSALIND: Yeah, I think that's probably typical.

AMY B.: Is that what you would recommend? Or do you think that would-be protégés should make an explicit ask?

ROSALIND: I would say that they probably should make an explicit ask, but only after the relationship has already been firmly established. I don't think this is one of those things where you go in and say, "Hey, I'm looking for a sponsor. Would you want to be my sponsor? And if you say yes, I promise that I'll work my hardest on the projects that you give me."

It's more that the protégé has to establish their credibility with the sponsor first. And they have to establish some sort of value proposition to a sponsor. Maybe that's by demonstrating their exceptional motivation or expertise in the areas that are highly relevant to what the sponsor cares about. But sponsors have to see in their own mind the capabilities of a protégé and believe that those outcomes are due primarily to the protégé's efforts; that's when the sponsor is going to say, "OK, I have such deep confidence in the capabilities of this individual that I am now ready to vouch for them to other people."

NICOLE: If there is someone who you have a good relationship with, and you think that they trust your competency, how do you ask them to sponsor you?

ROSALIND: I think it's about being really explicit about where you want to go and asking them for their advice on how to get there. That way, you're not saying, "I want your help." You're saying, "I'd like your advice on how to reach this goal." But in charting out that path, that then makes them have to think about the kind of concrete things that you could be doing. And then when those opportunities arise, they're more likely to think of you.

AMY GALLO: So it's more about making yourself available to be sponsored, or making it clear that you want to be sponsored, rather than saying, "Hey, will you be my sponsor?"

ROSALIND: One way is to focus on how protégés can make themselves more visible to sponsors. Another tactic that is relatively underexplored is how sponsors can understand what behaviors that they're engaging in that are particularly helpful. Are they treating employees systematically differently in terms of how they dole out those opportunities? And how are they determining who they decide they're going to advocate for versus who they won't advocate for?

For some—I'm thinking ethnic minorities and women—it's so difficult to get that social capital that you're a little more cautious about who you're willing to lend it to through sponsorship in case it might come back to be a bad decision. But I think there's a lot of work that could be done on men in terms of understanding how they could engage in sponsorship.

AMY G.: Let me ask about that, because your research shows that men are more effective sponsors of women than men. Why is that?

ROSALIND: The research indicates that male sponsors are more effective than female sponsors regardless of the gender of the person who's being sponsored. So if you're a woman working with a man, you're just as well off as a man working with a man. Comparatively speaking, female sponsors, regardless of whether or not the protégé is male or female, tend to be less effective—and by less effective, I mean their recommendations are seen as less credible and they're not as influential in actually getting the people that they recommend hired.

So why do I think that is? That is an excellent question that my doctoral student Elizabeth Campbell (I'm sponsoring her) and I are working on. We have found that tenure in the organization does seem to mitigate some of the hit that female sponsors take. The general gist is that women who are able to overcome the well-known gender discrimination in the promotion and retention process to achieve leadership positions are seen as especially competent. It's a phenomenon called the "female leader advantage." If you think about it in that light, then if the really senior woman is high-powered, super competent, and willing to recommend someone, it probably means that she sees a lot of value in them. So protégés of really senior women actually end up doing just as well as protégés of men. The big difference here is that you can be a relatively inexperienced male sponsor and still be really effective for your protégés, but if you're an inexperienced female sponsor, your protégés do not benefit from that.

AMY G.: So what's the takeaway on that for our listeners in terms of who they should be looking for to sponsor them? Men and high-powered women can be more effective. What's the lesson for people?

ROSALIND: I hesitate to give concrete recommendations about how to choose sponsors, because protégés don't choose sponsors. Sponsors choose protégés. And so for protégés to want to be strategic about it, I just don't think that there is necessarily one best tactic. I think you decide where you want to go and you make yourself indispensable to the people who are relevant to getting you to where you want to go. And they will typically take it from there.

Now, obviously, if you've been a real star performer but you don't feel as though you're getting the recognition you deserve, I think regardless of where you are, that's an opportunity to talk to your supervisor and to say, "Hey, I'd like to have a conversation about my future here in the organization. Can we talk together to chart a path forward?" And that's just a very natural way to have that frank, explicit conversation about your career goals and brainstorming and bringing them into the conversation about things they could do.

NICOLE: Can more junior female sponsors "cosponsor" a protégé with someone more senior? You told us earlier that you did that with your students. You "co-advised" them on their dissertations to bring in a senior person who had that social capital. Did you tell your students that you were doing that? Did you make that explicit?

ROSALIND: Yes. I did. It was a very explicit conversation—but in a way, it was apologetic! It was like, "I'm so sorry that I can't do this for you. And even though I know that I'm the one that you've primarily worked with, if we're resting your career on the basis of my recommendation, I worry that it's not going to go as far as I would like it to. And so the best way forward in my mind is to get someone else involved so that they can leverage their reputation on your behalf in a way that I won't be able to."

AMY B.: Are there moments when a sponsor should explicitly tell the protégé about work she's doing on their behalf? Are there times when that's inappropriate? Help us navigate that.

ROSALIND: I don't think that that needs to happen. You risk turning the relationship into a quid pro quo. I think what's most special about sponsorship relationships is that they are such close, personal relationships, not transaction-oriented relationships, where "I'm going to do something for you, and then you're going to do something for me." If a sponsor is constantly cataloging, "OK, I did this opportunity for you, so now I need you to do this for me," I feel like that would change the relationship in a way that would make the relationship less satisfactory to both parties.

AMY G.: So what we see is that you have to be strategic about what you share and what you don't. But if it's not explicit, how does the protégé even know that it's happening? One of the things I'm trying to wrap my head around is that it feels like you just put yourself out there—"Here are my career goals"—and then you hope someone leverages their influence for you. But where is this sort of accountability in all of this?

ROSALIND: That's an excellent question. People talk about having a sponsor, but you don't want just one. It's like any other resource in life. You should diversify, have more than one. I consider it like building your coalition of allies. Some of those people are going to end up being sponsors. Some of those people are not. But regardless of what you do, having allies, having supporters, is always important. And also you just don't know how those connections will end up becoming relevant.

It's just like networking. Really good networkers aren't going around and trying to find high-value propositions in the moment. That's not how they're thinking about the world. It's more like, "I'm going to get to know you, and I don't know how I might be useful for you or you might be useful for me at some point. You may not be useful for me right now, or I may not be useful for you at this moment. But there may come a time when the resource, knowledge, connections—whatever—become important. And so I'm just going to hold that in the deck and see what happens." I would approach sponsorship in very much the same kind of way.

. . .

NICOLE: Can we talk about a specific sponsorship moment involving Amy B. and myself? Because as I've reflected on sponsorship, I look back and see that, "Oh, I have been sponsored in the past." It was not something I went in asking for or that I thought about consciously. But this specific instance feels like a textbook case of what Rosalind was talking about. Amy B. and I got together one night, we were having a meeting, and she asked me, "Where do you want to be in the future, in five years?" And I said, "I want to be where you are. That's kind of the trajectory that I want to go towards— leading people and determining coverage." And she said, "Well, here's what you need to start doing. You need to start taking these opportunities. You need to manage. You need to do XYZ things." So I was doing the thing of saying, "Here's my vision for where I want to go." And then she had that in mind for, "This is kind of what Nicole's aspiring to."

And I think the next day, or a few days later, I found out that Amy had found an opportunity. She put me on a big editing project. And it was something I'd never done before. So that not only gave me the opportunity, it gave me the confidence to seize an opportunity to do something that I had no specific prior experience doing before.

AMY B.: Actually, I had not remembered that, that conversation, but here's what I do remember: I suddenly understood who Nicole wanted to be. And I knew who I thought she could be. And there was a lot of match there. And so, when she put it out there, what she wanted, it was easy to make a match. That's what it seemed like. I would never have asked her that initial question if I hadn't believed in her in a very big way. So it was not the formal, "Would you sponsor me?" or "May I sponsor you?" conversation. I think we'd both puke before we had that conversation.

NICOLE: We'd literally puke!

AMY B.: But, you know, it was a really honest moment of, "Tell me what you want," and when she had the guts to say what she wanted, it made it all very easy, from my perspective.

NICOLE: I would think that that is how a lot of sponsorship comes to be.

Rosalind Chow Answers Questions from Listeners About Sponsorship

How should one goes about thanking their sponsor? Am I showing enough thanks? Am I thanking too much? Am I showing enough excitement about having been helped?

—C.

First, there's no harm (as far as we know, based on the research) in expressing gratitude. If anything, people underestimate how meaningful it is to others to be thanked for their efforts, because most of us don't get thanked a lot! So if a person notices that I've gone out of my way to help them *and* they go out of their way to acknowledge my help, that usually builds a stronger relationship between us.

Now, there is a possibility that if women thank others too much, especially for things that are truly rather inconsequential, then they run the risk of implying "I can't do anything on my own without help." So one option is to thank the other person for providing the opportunity and discuss how you will or have already begun to execute and perform well, which means that they opened the door, but you're the one doing the work.

The other way to interpret the question is: Are there certain forms of sponsorship that are more worthy of appreciation than others? Again, giving thanks is always good, in my book. But taking the question at face value, I would suggest thinking about how much reputation your sponsor has put on the line for you. The more they had to actively insist on others' consideration of your abilities, the more "costly" that sponsorship is—and thus, more valuable. If someone says positive things about you in general, that's nice but not overly costly to them. But if they strategically introduce you to the other person and say, "This is the person I was telling you about! The one you should hire," that's a more active form of sponsorship that probably warrants a thank-you note.

It's one thing to have a sponsor, but then what? It's not always the smoothest ride; much of it is impacted by forces beyond your control, basically power struggles and office politics. What happens when your sponsor leaves the company and/or they get pushed out and you become collateral damage?

—G.

This relates to something I alluded to in the podcast: You don't want to have only one sponsor; like stocks, you need to diversify. The more senior you get, presumably, the more opportunity powerful people in the organization have to directly observe your talents, so you won't be as reliant on your sponsor.

But sometimes you pick the wrong horse (or the wrong horse picks you). Depending on what your relationship is with your sponsor, you can ask them for help and they can try transitioning you to another sponsor in the firm. You could also leave with your sponsor, assuming that they have found a position in another firm that you'd be interested in.

Adapted from "Sponsorship: Defining the Relationship," Women at Work *podcast season 4, episode 2, October 29, 2019.*

13

Sponsors Need to Stop Acting Like Mentors

by Julia Taylor Kennedy and Pooja Jain-Link

Sponsorship, or advocacy by senior leaders of rising talent, is a hot topic within corporate America. Deloitte's board chair, Mike Fucci, talks about it openly; Cisco has run a sponsorship pledge campaign called the "Multiplier Effect"; dozens of other companies have implemented sponsorship programs; and many (if not most) diversity and inclusion practitioners cite sponsorship as a key intervention to diversify top leadership.

But something is keeping sponsorship from working. In our research at Coqual (formerly the Center for Talent Innovation), we found that sponsors themselves don't really understand the role and how to do it well.[1] This insight came out of a nationally representative survey of over 3,000 U.S. professionals across many career levels.

In our survey, we asked respondents whether they are sponsors, what they do for their protégés, and what their protégés do for them, which helped us understand sponsors' investments and their dividends.

We discovered that many who consider themselves to be sponsors are acting more like mentors. To claim the title of sponsor, a senior leader should be an active advocate for their protégé—a more junior professional who the sponsor sees as a top performer, with tons of potential, who deserves to move up in their career. A sponsor has three primary responsibilities: to believe in and go out on a limb for their protégé; to use their organizational capital, both publicly and behind closed doors, to push for their protégé's promotion; and to provide their protégé with "air cover" for risk-taking. This means shielding the protégé from critics and naysayers as they explore out-of-the box ideas and work on stretch assignments to set them apart from peers. Yet only 27% of our survey respondents who identified as sponsors said they advocate for their protégé's promotion. Even fewer (19%) reported providing their protégé with air cover.

We also found evidence of "mini-me" syndrome— sponsors reported a tendency to select protégés who reminded them of themselves. A full 71% of self-identified sponsors said that their protégé shares their same gender or race. This isn't all that surprising, given that unconscious affinity biases drive us to seek the company of individuals who make us feel comfortable: those who share our race, gender, upbringing, culture, religion, and so on. But this kind of selection presents a roadblock to wider-spread sponsorship for underrepresented groups. White male leadership—still a clear majority in corporate America—self-perpetuates, while diverse talent is kept outside of the C-suite.

One way sponsors can break the mini-me pattern is to prioritize difference—perhaps a unique skill set or distinct personal brand—as they consider potential protégés. When a protégé brings complementary talents to the table, they can expand a sponsor's capacity to deliver, open doors to new networks and markets, and contribute a valuable management style to the team. Yet sponsors simply aren't focused on this. Only 23% of sponsors in our survey said they look for potential protégés with skills or management styles that they do not have themselves.

Another important finding was that even when practiced imperfectly, sponsorship still carries dividends. Sponsors in our sample were more likely than non-sponsors to report being satisfied with their own advancement, being engaged at work, being able to deliver on "mission impossible" projects, and having a bench of talent that expands their skill sets. This makes sense. When a professional begins to cultivate an "A-team" of protégés, they can be more effective, more efficient, and signal to themselves and senior leaders that they're ready for the next step in their career.

To understand the full dividends of good sponsorship, we conducted several interviews with top business leaders who speak openly about the role sponsorship has played in their own success. We wanted to get a more intimate insight into the sponsor/protégé dynamic, and we asked for detailed examples of times executives benefited from performing the role of a sponsor, especially on behalf of protégés with different backgrounds from their own. Two important examples of what they'd gained from sponsoring stood out.

You can build deep trust with your protégés—and get honest, unvarnished feedback from them

As Booz Allen Hamilton's CEO, Horacio Rozanski, told us, most of the feedback he gets has "so much bubble-wrap around it you can't tell exactly what's inside." He craves straight talk, and he gets it from his protégé Jen Wagner. Initially, Rozanski decided to advocate for her because she shares his values. "I don't need to know people socially to feel comfortable sponsoring them," he said. "But I do need to know they stand for the same things that I do."

When he met Wagner, he knew she was smart and driven—all of his colleagues at a certain level are, he points out—but what struck him was her tenacity and ability to rein in big egos, traits she developed in part as a single parent. After asking around and confirming her integrity from colleagues, Rozanski knew Wagner would make a worthy protégé. When he was appointed COO, he selected Wagner to serve in a newly created position, director of operations, that required a high level of skill. This move solidified their intense bond of trust. He wanted to propel Wagner's career while hewing to the company's merit-based culture. He helped Wagner become acquainted with other high-powered executives so they too would see her value to the company when a promotion became available or it was time for a pay raise. Now, as a senior vice president, she continues to report directly to Rozanski, which gives her many opportunities to deliver that feedback that's so hard for him to come by.

Your protégés—and your commitment to sponsorship—can extend your legacy

When former EY U.S. Chairman and Managing Partner and EY Americas Managing Partner Steve Howe retired, he left behind more than a legacy of great work. Through his work with countless protégés, he left in his wake a cadre of leaders to carry his approach, which includes promoting sponsorship, forward.

"I knew [sponsorship] helped me, and so as I took on more responsibility, I realized that that investment in sponsorship was going to be important to others," Howe reflects. "I tried to take that on myself and then to build it into our culture in a meaningful way that our people would understand it and invest in it—both those being sponsored and those doing the sponsoring."

Howe met one of his many protégés, Kate Barton, when she was in her first management role with the company. When she was passed over for an anticipated promotion, Howe took the time to reassure her that he, and the company, recognized her value; when the job again became vacant, he coached her on how she could influence the board and win the spot. Through this process, he earned Barton's loyalty to himself as her advocate, and her loyalty to EY, an organization she felt confident would support her career development. Howe gained a protégé he could trust, and one who understood the value of going out on a limb to keep great talent engaged at EY.

Now in her 33rd year at EY, Barton serves as the global lead of Tax Services. She has taken on many protégés of her own, and even worked alongside Howe to sponsor junior employees. "We're all about legacy," Barton shared. "That's what Steve created, and that's what I want to do as well."

It's wonderful that sponsorship has taken root in the business world's zeitgeist. But rather than close the book, it's time to push harder to ensure sponsors, protégés, and organizations all understand this crucial relationship and its nuanced dynamics. When both protégés and sponsors recognize the benefits of playing their roles right, and of partnering across lines of difference, sponsorship's potential to bring deserving employees of all identities into leadership can finally be realized.

Adapted from content posted on hbr.org, September 26, 2019 (product #H04TFG).

14

Make Yourself Sponsor-Worthy

by Sylvia Ann Hewlett

Maggie says, "I've always given 110%." "Whoever I worked for, I gave them my all, every day, 10 hours a day, weekends and holidays, whatever it took. That endeared me to a lot of powerful men."

That dedication and loyalty should have made Maggie a star. Yet although she rose in the organization, because she wasn't strategic about whom she gave her 110% to, she squandered her gifts on leaders who didn't invest in her. Without a sponsor to spotlight her attributes, offer her opportunities, and kick her career into high gear, she found herself stuck for years in what she calls "permanent lieutenant syndrome."

Maggie was eventually fortunate enough to find a sponsor and today is an executive at a global financial advisory firm with 22,000 people reporting to her. But there are thousands of Maggies out there—hardworking, devoted, consistent performers toiling in relative obscurity. How can you break out of the pack and attract a sponsor?

Rather than hoping for a lucky break, focus your energies by making yourself sponsor-worthy. To begin with, you must come through on two obvious fronts: performance and loyalty.

When asked how she had built great relationships with three different sponsors, Sian McIntyre, head of Legal at Lloyd's Banking Group, says simply, "I've delivered." She hit her targets and deadlines, executed brilliantly on her assignments, and produced outstanding bottom-line results. "They all felt the benefit of that," McIntyre notes, "and wanted me on board for subsequent projects."

Loyalty manifests in many different ways: trust that's earned through repeated demonstration of a dedicated work ethic, commitment to a shared mission, and allegiance to the firm. Winning a sponsor's trust doesn't require becoming a toady. On the contrary, showing that you can ultimately be entrusted with a leadership position depends on demonstrating that you will stand up to them when necessary.

Tiger Tyagarajan, CEO of Genpact, attributes his success to the bond he cultivated with Pramod Bhasin, his boss and sponsor for 17 years. Because of a deep trust built on shared values, Bhasin would listen when Tiger pushed back. "I'd say, 'Here's my logic on this,' and show him that I understood his logic but also show him why it wouldn't work. He was amenable to that as long as I kept it private," Tiger recalls. "We had very different styles, and sometimes we simply agreed to disagree. But in the end, I think that what he valued in me was the very thing that complemented him."

But performance and loyalty are not enough to get a sponsor's notice, let alone convince them to invest in you. You'll need to differentiate yourself from your peers. You'll need to develop and deploy a personal brand. You'll need to do *something* or be *someone* who can extend a sponsor's reach and influence by adding distinct value.

What do *you* bring to the table?

Some protégés add value through their technical expertise or social media savvy. Others derive an enduring identity through fluency in another language or culture. Consider acquiring skills that your job doesn't require but that set you apart—and make you a stronger contributor to a team. For example, Tiger Tyagarajan had a special ability to build teams from scratch and coach raw talent—an invaluable asset that was key as the firm transitioned from a startup into a multinational infotech giant. One 25-year-old sales rep, noting that her potential sponsor Tiger "wasn't exactly current in terms of the internet," took pains to brief her on job candidates whose résumés bristled with technical jargon and references to social media innovation that she simply couldn't understand, let alone assess for relevance. "I just helped educate her so she didn't come off as some kind of dinosaur," says the rep, whose tactful teaching gained her a powerful promoter.

Lastly, don't be shy about your successes. Alert potential sponsors to your valuable assets. Since it can be difficult to toot your own horn, work with peers to sing each other's praises. A VP at Merrill Lynch described how she and three other women, all high-potential leaders in different divisions of the firm, would meet monthly for lunch to update each other on their projects and accomplishments. The idea was to be ready to talk each other up, should an occasion arise. "So if my boss were to complain about some problem he's struggling to solve, I could say, 'You know, you should talk to Lisa in Global Equities, because she's had a lot of experience with that,'" this VP explained. "It turned out to be a really effective tactic, because we could be quite compelling about each other's accomplishments." In short order, all four women acquired sponsors and were promoted.

Finding the right person to highlight your accomplishments and push you to the top is a hard task, but it's necessary if you want to break out of the "permanent lieutenant" doldrums. Just doing good work isn't enough. Take the first step and make yourself not only a hard worker but an emerging leader worthy of a sponsor.

Adapted from content posted on hbr.org, February 6, 2014 (product #H00NIB).

15

Don't Underestimate the Power of Women Supporting Each Other at Work

by Anne Welsh McNulty

As my experiences from being a rookie accountant to a managing director at an investment bank have taught me, conversations between women have massive benefits for the individual and the organization. When I graduated college in the 1970s, I believed that women would quickly achieve parity at all levels of professional life now that we had "arrived"— I viewed the lack of women at the top as more of a "pipeline" problem, not a cultural one. But the support I expected to find from female colleagues—the feeling of sisterhood in this mission—rarely survived first contact within the workplace.

When I was a first-year accountant at a Big Eight firm (now the Big Four), I kept asking the only woman senior to me to go to lunch, until finally she told me, "Look, there's only room for one female partner here. You and I are not going to be friends." Unfortunately, she was acting rationally. Senior-level women who champion younger women even today are more likely to get negative performance reviews, according to a 2016 study in the *Academy of Management Journal*.[1]

My brusque colleague's behavior has a (misogynistic) academic name: the "Queen Bee" phenomenon. Some senior-level women distance themselves from junior women, perhaps to be more accepted by their male peers. As a study published in the *Leadership Quarterly* concludes, this is a *response* to inequality at the top, not the cause.[2] Trying to separate oneself from a marginalized group is, sadly, a strategy that's frequently employed. It's easy to believe that there's limited space for people who look like you at the top when you can see it with your own eyes.

By contrast, men are 46% more likely to have a higher-ranking advocate in the office, according to economist Sylvia Ann Hewlett. This makes an increasing difference in representation as you go up the org chart. According to a 2016 McKinsey report, *Women in the Workplace*, white men make up 36% of entry-level corporate jobs and white women make up 31%.[3] But at the very first rung above that, those numbers change to 47% for white men and 26% for white women—a 16% drop. For women of color, the drop from 17% to 11% is a plunge of 35%. People tend to think that whatever conditions exist now are "normal." Maybe this (charitably) explains men's blind spots: At companies where only 1 in 10 senior leaders are women, according to McKinsey, nearly 50% of men felt that women were "well represented" in leadership.

Worse than being snubbed by the woman above me was the lack of communication between women at my level. Of the 50 auditors in my class, five were women. All of us were on different client teams. At the end of my first year, I was shocked and surprised to learn that all four of the other women had quit or been fired—shocked at the outcome, and surprised because we hadn't talked among ourselves enough to understand what was happening. During that year, I'd had difficult experiences with men criticizing me, commenting on my looks, or flatly saying I didn't deserve to work there—but I had no idea that the other women were having similar challenges. We expected our performance to be judged as objectively as our clients' books, and we didn't realize the need to band together until it was too late. Each of us had dealt with those challenges individually, and obviously not all successfully.

I resolved not to let either of those scenarios happen again; I wanted to be aware of what was going on with the women I worked with. As I advanced in my career,

I hosted women-only lunches and created open channels of communication. I made it a point to reach out to each woman who joined the firm with an open-door policy, sharing advice and my personal experiences, including how to say no to doing traditionally gendered (and uncompensated) tasks like getting coffee or taking care of the office environment. To personal assistants, who might find some of those tasks unavoidable, I emphasized that they could talk to me about any issues in the workplace, that their roles were critical, and that they should be treated with respect. The lunches were essential, providing a dedicated space to share challenges and successes. Coming together as a group made people realize that their problems weren't just specific to them, but in fact were collective obstacles. All of this vastly improved the flow of information and relieved tension and anxiety. It reassured us that though our jobs were challenging, we were not alone. In doing so, I hope it lowered the attrition rate of women working at my company—rates that are, across all corporate jobs, stubbornly higher for women than men, especially women of color.

My own daughter has arrived to a workplace that has not changed nearly as much as I had hoped—although 40% of Big Four accounting firm employees are women, they make up only 19% of audit partners. Only one in five C-suite members is a woman, and they are still less likely than their male peers to report that there are equal opportunities for advancement.

So what are women in the workplace to do, when research shows that we're penalized for trying to lift each other up? The antidote to being penalized for sponsoring women may just be to do it more—and to do it vocally, loudly, and proudly—until we're able to change perceptions. There are massive benefits for the individual and the organization when women support each other. The advantages of sponsorship for protégés may be clear, such as access to opportunities and having their achievements brought to the attention of senior management; but sponsors gain as well, by becoming known as cultivators of talent and as leaders. Importantly, organizations that welcome such sponsorship benefit too—creating a culture of support, where talent is recognized and rewarded for all employees. Sponsorship (which involves connecting a protégé with opportunities and contacts and advocating on their behalf, as opposed to the more advice-focused role of mentorship) is also an excellent way for men to be allies at work.

But there's still so much work that needs to be done. I'm thrilled by the rise of women's organizations like Sallie Krawchek's Ellevate Network, a professional network of women supporting each other across companies to change the culture of business at large. (I'm especially fond of it because it began as "85 Broads," a network of Goldman alumnae that drew its name from the old GS headquarters address before Krawcheck, a Merrill alumna, bought and expanded it.) That network spawned a sibling, Ellevest, an investment firm focused on women and companies that advance women. Other ventures include Dee Poku-Spalding's WIE (Women Inspiration and Enterprise) networks, whose mission is to support women in their career ambitions by providing real-world learning via access to established business leaders. I am attempting to make my own dent in this area, having endowed the McNulty Institute for Women's Leadership at my alma mater, Villanova, which supports new research and leadership development opportunities for women.

These are wonderful supplements, but they can't replace the benefits of and the necessity for connections among women inside a company—at and across all levels. It reduces the feeling of competition for an imaginary quota at the top. It helps other women realize, "Oh, it's not just me"—a revelation that can change the course of a woman's career. It's also an indispensable way of identifying bad actors and systemic problems within the company. It need not be a massive program, and you don't need to overthink it—in fact, there's a healthy debate about affinity groups run from the top down. Whether you are a first-year employee or a manager, just reach out and make those connections. I'm guessing you'll find that the return on investment on the cost of a group lunch will be staggering.

Adapted from content posted on hbr.org, September 3, 2018 (product #H04HSC).

16

Want to Be a Better Manager? Get a Protégé

by Sylvia Ann Hewlett

W ho benefits when a manager or executive sponsors someone more junior, offering guidance, advocacy, and support? If you answered, *the protégé*, you'd be only getting it half right.

Sponsorship—a relationship in which an established or rising leader picks an outstanding junior talent and develops that person's career—certainly does boost the protégé, who has access to the sponsor's experience and connections. But data shows that the sponsor also gains enormous value from this relationship. According to a nationally representative survey conducted for my book, *The Sponsor Effect: How to Be a Better Leader by Investing in Others,* senior-level managers who have a protégé are 53% more likely to report having received a promotion in the previous two years. Entry-level managers who have a protégé are 60% more likely to have received a stretch assignment.

Looking at the long term, among survey respondents—who ranged from entry-level managers to CEOs—39% of those with a protégé deemed themselves "satisfied with their professional legacies" at this moment of their careers. Only 25% of those who didn't have protégés said the same.

The benefits of sponsorship don't accrue to managers and executives who merely *mentor* someone more junior. A mentor offers advice and perhaps an introduction or two; the mentee listens politely and says thank you. Sponsor and protégé, on the other hand, are both actively and publicly *working* for each other's success. It's that active investment from both sides that makes the relationship so mutually beneficial.

Consider Lou Aversano, Chief Client Officer, Worldwide, of Oligvy (a division of WPP) in New York. Aversano is already high up in the advertising world—but it's a world with increasingly shaky foundations. As consumers have gone digital and mobile, and as traditional clients want alternatives to keeping firms on long-term retainers, ad agencies have had to reinvent themselves.

"You have to be willing to burn your lifeboats before someone burns them for you," Aversano said about the industry in a conversation with me. Yet he admits that it's often hard for veterans, who built their success the old-fashioned way, to come up with ideas to change it all up. "We see things from a certain height, and we have biases based on our legacy," he said.

For Aversano, the answer was a protégé: a younger talent he would personally invest in and on whom he could count for performance, loyalty, and a new view of the ad world. To find that protégé, he tapped Ogilvy's Young Professionals Network. He and other senior leaders worked with its 100 members (with an average age of 27) on ideas to transform the agency—and they observed and guided these young employees closely. It took time, but Aversano found the talent he was looking for: a young man named Ben Levine. Levine has since helped Aversano create a new staffing structure, a new path to growth, and (for both Aversano personally and the firm) a conduit to a younger generation's ways of thinking and working.

Protégés don't have to be younger than you or a fresh face in the industry. What defines a good protégé is that they work effectively and loyally for you, and they have the ability to expand your worldview or skill set. That last part usually means someone who differs from you in gender, ethnicity, sexual orientation, professional background, management style, or life experience. I've seen, for example, sponsors gain access to new markets through a protégé who understands women's healthcare priorities, Latin American cultural sensibilities, or the LGBTQ community's financial planning needs; I've also seen men and women rise to become CEOs of giant enterprises with the help of protégés who loyally extend their reach and fill their knowledge and skill gaps.

Of course, sponsorship does involve risk. Miscommunication can occur, especially when your protégés are (as they often should be) different from you. It can also be tricky not to let the relationship take up too much time—it must be your protégé who does most of the work. Then there's the risk of a protégé in whom you've publicly invested time, responsibilities, and reputational capital letting you down by failing to grow the bottom line, impress important stakeholders, or take work off your shoulders. Some protégés even betray their sponsor's trust, causing immense damage.

But done right, the benefits of having a more junior talent who loyally works on your behalf, performing tasks for which you lack the time, skills, or inclination, are simply too great to ignore. Savvy sponsors therefore act to mitigate the risks—and maximize the benefits of a significant investment of time and their personal brand—by following seven steps:

1. **Identify.** Know what to look for in potential protégés, starting with performance and trustworthiness.

2. **Include.** Look for protégés who are different from you, whether in mindset (often from having a different domain of knowledge or belonging to

a different generation) or in gender, ethnicity, or sexual orientation.

3. **Inspire.** Ensure that your protégés align with your values, and use their ambitions to spur them forward.

4. **Instruct.** Help your protégés fill their gaps, whether in hard knowledge or soft skills.

5. **Inspect.** Continuously evaluate to confirm that your protégés are delivering both performance and trustworthiness.

6. **Instigate a deal.** When you are confident that value is being delivered, make the ask and spell out the terms of this reciprocal relationship.

7. **Invest in three ways.** Go all in with capital, clout, and cover. Endorse and advocate vigorously for your protégés and provide air cover when they need it.

Whether you're a mid-level manager looking to make your name or a senior executive looking to expand your productivity and reach, a protégé can be the answer. When managed carefully, the relationship will help both of you rise and thrive.

Adapted from content posted on hbr.org, June 17, 2019 (product #H050IM).

17

What Men Can Do to Be Better Mentors and Sponsors to Women

by Rania H. Anderson and David G. Smith

Advocating for women's advancement at work is integral for improving financial results, gender balance, and diversity in our workplaces and leadership teams. Yet data from the Working Mother Research Institute finds that while 48% of men say they have received detailed information on career paths to P&L jobs in the past 24 months, just 15% of women report the same.[1] And, while 54% of men had a career discussion with a mentor or sponsor in the past 24 months, only 39% of women did.

Why? Because leaders, the majority of whom are male and white, don't adequately sponsor or mentor people who don't look like them. Recent research from the

Center for Talent Innovation reported that a full 71% of executives have protégés whose gender and race match their own.[2] That means that women and minorities don't benefit from sponsorship like their male colleagues do, and organizations lose out by not gaining the full potential of diverse talent.

Confusion about the #MeToo movement may have unintentionally exacerbated the situation. Two 2018 surveys by Lean In and Bloomberg Media found that, in the wake of those high-profile workplace sexual harassment and assault allegations, some men began to avoid professional work relationships with women.[3] It was even a topic at a recent World Economic Forum: senior male executives talked about avoiding one-on-one mentoring relationships as a risk management strategy.

This response is not productive. There are plenty of men who want to do what's best for their businesses and employees. We find that sponsorship and advocacy make the biggest difference.

Sponsors, by definition, use their position and power to achieve business objectives by advancing a protégé's career. They are not benevolent benefactors. They are influential leaders who intentionally invest in, and rely on, the skills and contributions of their protégés to achieve their own goals and their protégés' highest potential. Sponsors need to know the skills and capabilities of their protégés, see their potential, and be able to orchestrate their advancement—but they don't have to show them how to play the instrument or encourage them to practice.

And while mentors may or may not have the same level of power as sponsors, they frequently have a great deal more influence than they actually use. We regularly see mentors who support their mentees privately but are reluctant to advocate for them.

If companies truly want to improve their financial results and diversity, they need to do a better job of developing sponsors for diverse talent at all levels of their organization. Leaders are regularly taught about strategic thinking, championing change, making financial decisions, and managing people, but they are not taught how to become sponsors or maximize their impact in the role. As a result, white men don't have the skills to advance women and people of color—even though they unconsciously help other white men to do so. Rather than be frustrated by or blame male leaders, companies need to better enlist and equip them to excel. And men need to consistently implement what they learn.

All of this starts with understanding what the best sponsors do, and how they do it. Here are the eight key steps we've identified based on our experiences advising global leaders and companies.

Identify high-potential diverse talent

Great sponsors purposefully look for people who bring different experiences and perspectives from their own and also have the results, potential, and ambition to make a larger contribution. If they can't identify someone on their own, they go out of their way to ask HR and other leaders to recommend candidates.

One of Rania's coaching clients, Stan, an executive director of a regional bank, is a great example of this type of sponsor. He recognized the potential in one of his employees, Beth. Even though she had no prior financial services experience when she joined the bank, she was great at developing client, community, and internal relationships. Stan could see that, if she held a senior leadership role, she could make a broader contribution. He decided to sponsor her to fast-track her into a senior market role.

Determine the best stretch role

It is vital to identify high-visibility opportunities that could benefit from your protégés' perspectives, talents, and experiences—and in which they can excel. These should be roles or projects that, if executed successfully, will clearly benefit the business as well their career. The best opportunities to develop protégés are those that meet some of these conditions: involves profit and loss;

high risk; strategic clients; strategic importance to the business; starting something new; or fixing a business problem. Stan did this by recognizing that Beth's management skills would make a notable improvement in their market's retail division.

Similarly, when Jay, an executive at a fast-growth financial services startup, recognized that Lexi had the talent to achieve more significant results and advance, he assigned her several complex business challenges that required her to interact with senior leaders across the organization. After she successfully addressed them, she gained positive visibility.

Position the role

Stretch assignments can be challenging, so great sponsors ensure that their protégés understand that the organization values and thinks highly of them. Many women want and appreciate this type of encouragement and may be reticent to take a challenging role without it. Protégés should be provided with context on the importance of new opportunities, what a sponsor believes they can accomplish, and how the sponsor and the company will support them. Have their manager and mentors encourage them to persist in spite of the obstacles they will inevitably encounter. In Stan's case, he talked to Beth about why he thought she'd excel in leading the retail banking group and what success in that role could mean her for her in the future.

Provide opportunities for development and support

Sponsors must ensure that people in their organization invest time, expertise, resources, and budget to help give protégés the skills and experiences they need to be successful. This is where mentors and other advisers come in. As Beth demonstrated results, Stan arranged for her to have technical skill and leadership development experiences. Both Beth and Lexi were provided with executive leadership coaching.

It's also important to educate leaders who will work with a protégé about the challenges women, people of color, and especially women of color often encounter in the workplace. It's also worth exploring if a protégé can be connected with people in similar life and career stages or those who have had prior success navigating through personal and professional challenges.

Pave the way

Sponsors have a responsibility to introduce their protégés to influential and powerful people in their organization or industry, including clients, especially if they are crucial for success in their work. In Lexi's case, this meant having her travel internationally to meet with key partners and an important leadership role assignment on a transition team. She delivered stellar results. In both

Beth's and Lexi's cases, their sponsor regularly communicated their results and advocated for them with other senior executives.

Ensure that protégés receive candid, performance-based feedback

A 2016 McKinsey study found that women don't get the same type of direct, candid commentary on their performance as their male counterparts, and research shows that women consistently receive less feedback tied to business outcomes.[4] Sponsors may or may not be the people who provide protégés with this. But they must make sure that protégés get clear performance assessments that include specific guidance to help improve results and promote advancement. For example, instead of feedback like "Be more assertive," an example of actionable feedback is: "When the client raises these types of objections, acknowledge their concerns but come back in with specific examples of other clients for whom these factors have not been an issue. This will help you close more business."

Help protégés persist

No matter the stretch assignment, there will always be challenges and setbacks. Sponsors must make sure criticism, mistakes, failures, or naysayers don't derail their protégés. That doesn't mean sheltering them from adversity; it does mean ensuring that the organization is understanding and patient if everything doesn't work out the first time. More often than not, success takes more than one assignment.

Champion promotions and recognition

Sponsors advocate for raises, promotions, and recognition to deserving protégés. As Beth delivered, Stan gave her additional responsibilities which have prepared her for a significant promotion. Lexi recently advanced into a senior leadership role. It took her excellent performance, advocating for herself, and Jay's advocacy to the rest of his executive committee teammates.

Our experience and the data show that women receive less sponsorship and advocacy in mentorship than their male colleagues. This imbalance is one of the primary reasons they don't advance at the same pace as men and why they leave their places of employment.

Leaders who take these steps will become better, more inclusive sponsors, which will improve their own results, the careers of protégés, and the organizations in which they work. Gender balance in companies and on teams improves a host of outcomes including financial results, innovation, decision-making, organizational commitment, retention, and job satisfaction. And managers who identify and develop all high-potential talent are more successful and recognized for this approach.

Companies can encourage this kind of sponsorship by clearly defining the steps, behaviors, and expectations for people in formal programs. They can deliberately address the mandate and process for advocacy and sponsorship of diverse talent in their employee development programs and performance assessments. And, finally, they hold senior managers accountable for sponsorship. It is not only good for women and people of color; it's also good for business and for the sponsors.

Adapted from content posted on hbr.org, August 7, 2019 (reprint #H0525R).

Making Work Friendships Work

18

Work Friendships Are Mostly Amazing and Sometimes Messy

A conversation with Nancy Rothbard
and Julianna Pillemer

t's great to have colleagues who are also friends. They can make coming to work more fun and engaging and can even make a ho-hum job more tolerable. It's a good feeling when we have someone to cheer us on, to confide in, be straight with, to cry in front of. But they also involve challenges, like maintaining those friendships when you become a boss or trying to tone down a relationship that's just too draining.

Nancy Rothbard, a professor at the University of Pennsylvania's Wharton School, and Julianna Pillemer, a professor at New York University's Stern School of Business, are researchers who have studied work friendships. *Women at Work* cohosts Amy Bernstein and Nicole Torres sat down

The Upsides of Work Friendship

AMY GALLO: Can we talk about the upsides of work friends?

AMY BERNSTEIN: Because they're so good.

AMY G.: Because there's so many good upsides.

AMY B.: They make work fun and they reinforce what's good about work for you.

NICOLE: Yeah. They get you excited about coming in each day. I get so much energy from friends at work because we have amazing conversations about things we're excited about, ideas that we have—and it's just fun. It's such a good break to have those throughout the day. It helps me stay productive and it helps maintain my energy.

with them to discuss how friends can set boundaries and get past stressful moments at work.

NICOLE TORRES: One question we hear a lot is where "work friendship" separates from "real friendship." From what you see in your research, where are the boundaries?

NANCY ROTHBARD: There are a lot of things that set workplace friendships apart from other types of friend-

AMY B.: And the real friends that you have, the ones who are really rooting for you, they can give you so much sustenance when you're feeling tired or a little blue. They really can just change the channel for you in your head.

AMY G.: Yeah. I don't come to the office all that often, and one of my friends here, when I've been gone for a while, will leave candy on my desk. It's just the sweetest thing. And usually I'm coming into a day full of meetings and stressed out, and then there's a Twix on my chair, and it makes me so happy.

AMY B.: That's really sweet.

AMY G.: I know. They're the best.

ships. But I also want to say that work friendships can be real friendships also; they're just slightly different. One of the key differentiators is that work relationships are sometimes not voluntary. Often, you have to see this person every day, whether you like them or not. In other types of friendships, you are usually free to choose whether you associate with them. A second differentiator is there's an expectation that work has a formality to it, whereas in friendship relationships, informality is often central. Another is that the key goals for a friendship are not instrumental or task-oriented—they're socioemotional goals. Finally, the norms at work for how we interact with one another are more exchange-based and less communal than in typical friendships.

NICOLE: What have you learned in studying workplace friendships? What are the good things that come from them and what are the bad things, if there are any?

JULIANNA PILLEMER: We're always very careful to say that we don't think work friendships are bad. We came at this research thinking that friendships at work are inevitable, and Nancy raised questions about the kind of tensions that can occur when a work friendship comes up against the requirements of being a good employee. One example is when you are in a meeting and you want to support your friend, but you actually disagree with them. What are the ways in which that can play out? You have to consider your role as a friend versus your role as an employee. Another thing is the impact your friendship can have on others. You may be thinking, "Oh, wow—I feel really great in this friendship. It's so great to have this emotional support." But in our research, we look at the way that that friendships like this can affect the people outside of those relationships and make them feel really excluded and left out.

NANCY: There are a couple of key outcomes that we look at. One is the individual outcomes: If I'm friends with somebody at work, there are some positive things that happen for me individually. I feel less lonely, I feel more connected, I have a lot more socioemotional support, and those are all good things. But it can also lead to the risk of me being distracted from my tasks at work. And if I'm getting a lot of socioemotional support from my friend, I'm probably having to reciprocate that socioemotional support. That might be distracting at certain key moments when I might need to be focusing on other parts of my job.

A second piece, which is related to what Julianna talked about earlier, is that when we're friends with somebody in the same work group, we may feel uncomfortable disagreeing with them, even when it's necessary for the betterment of the organization. To hash out the details of a problem, the team may need divergent viewpoints.

NICOLE: Can you give us some practical advice for how you manage conflicts that arise in your work friendships? How do you handle these tensions that you talked about? What are some effective strategies for managing them so you preserve your friendships but you also don't feel like you're giving up something at work?

JULIANNA: Just awareness that downsides can occur, just having those conversations very early on in the friendship, even before conflict can arise—that alone can help to mitigate some of those threats.

NANCY: That could look like Julianna and me talking about how I'm there for her but that I also really need my space to focus sometimes because that's how I need to work. It's almost like setting up a contract or an expectation with your friend up front about what your priorities are and what you need in order to be able to get your work done effectively.

If you are in a hierarchical friendship, it is also important to be transparent about the decision-making processes. Julianna was my doctoral student, and we're friends. There's a hierarchical divide there, so how do we navigate that? How do I make sure that the other PhD students, who know that we're friendly, don't think that I'm favoring Julianna? Those are the kinds of things that were on our minds as we were writing this paper.

NICOLE: So how did you navigate that hierarchical difference? How did you make sure that none of your other students felt like you were playing favorites?

NANCY: I don't know. Was I successful, Julianna?

JULIANNA: I don't know if you were successful. [LAUGHTER] I don't know. It's impossible, I think.

NANCY: We think we were successful, but it would really be the other people who would have to tell us. What I would say is I kept to very high standards of expectation about the work that she was producing. Also, she had a co-adviser on her dissertation. So that really helped too, I think, to make sure that people knew that it wasn't just me who was evaluating her.

AMY BERNSTEIN: So one of our listeners sent us this question, and I'd love to share it with you and get your thoughts. She says, *In my current job, I learned the hard way about being a manager and befriending an employee. I grew extremely close to an employee, opened up personally as well as professionally, and built her up to rise the corporate ladder with me. I had her back when others didn't and fought for her. I even welcomed her into my home. She ended up putting in her two weeks' notice via email to me, and I was crushed. I learned quickly that in a new managerial role, I could not get too close to my employees and had to take the emotion out of it.* What are your thoughts on that?

JULIANNA: This makes me think of some research we have seen that looks at the emotional help managers give. Managers may view this as really putting themselves out there, while employees sometimes can view the same interactions as "You're doing your job as a manager." So there's some complexity here around the employee simply feeling like the manager was doing her job in mentoring her. From her point of view, she was still within her rights to do what was best for her from a career perspective.

This gets at interesting hierarchical dynamics, but it also speaks to the fuzzy boundary and uncertainty around where your work friendship ends and where your role as employee or mentor begins. I would encourage the writer to perhaps adjust her expectations or try to understand this employee's perspective, that he or she might not have thought that this was a friendship or not been sure about the nature of that relationship. There is always that uncertainty around relational definitions when they occur at work.

NICOLE: We also got some questions from listeners about *not* having friends at work and even losing friends at work. We heard from incredibly close friends who had to work through one of them leaving their job and so no longer working together. Could you talk to us about coping with loneliness, whether it's because you don't have friends at work that you're close to or whether it's because someone—a close friend of yours—at your job has left, and all of a sudden you're alone and don't have that workplace friend. How do you deal with that?

NANCY: Our colleague Sigal Barsade has a paper on loneliness at work called "No Employee an Island." And one of the things that she finds is that a key predictor that reduces loneliness at work is having at least one friend at work. You don't have to have a lot of friends at work, but you should have somebody that you feel connected to deeply on some additional level. And what happens when that person leaves? So it's probably important that you have more than one friend at work so that you can guard against that loneliness really hitting you at that point.

JULIANNA: And if there's not that opportunity at work, just being sure that you have the support around you in your life to cope with that. I think there's always going to be a challenge for people who want to find these close relationships at work, because there might be someone who they think is really great who just doesn't value work friendship as much or thinks, "Yeah, of course when I leave, I'm not going to stay in touch with you." With people spending more and more time at work, it's easy to get your whole identity wrapped up in that. Being sure that you maintain some of yourself that's outside of that domain is really important. Psychologists call this "self-complexity." If you put all of your eggs in this work basket from a relational standpoint, that loneliness is going to hit you a lot harder.

NICOLE: What happens when a work friendship goes off the rails? You're too distracted or it's too emotionally draining, and those things are getting in the way of your job—you need to cut this friendship off. Have you ever experienced that? And what do you do?

NANCY: A lot of times where I've seen that happen has been where a hierarchical difference has arisen, where people were peers and then one of them is promoted and the other person has a really hard time dealing with that. And they can't necessarily leave. So the way people deal with it is through a lot of silence, simmering.

AMY B.: Cold war. What about getting a work relationship back on the rails after there's a rupture? How do you do that?

NANCY: It's really hard. One of the things that the trust literature talks about is that trust is really easy to lose really hard to regain. It takes a lot of work to rebuild a ruptured relationship, but sometimes you can do it out of necessity. You see that person all the time and you know what you have to do is lay what happened out on the table and try to be open to what their perspective is on it. When any relationship goes wrong—and this certainly applies to workplace relationships—it's often the case that we are really thinking about our own perspective on the situation and the other person is thinking about *their* own perspective. You each have to acknowledge that you had a part in it too and be willing to acknowledge that you did something wrong as well. Otherwise you can't restore that relationship.

Usually there has to be a pretty strong incentive to do so, like you are going to be on a consulting team and you're going to spend the next eight weeks with this person every day. It's hard to ghost them when you have to work with them and see them every day like that.

JULIANNA: I think Nancy's point about being real and putting it all on the table is interesting. This idea of, How much of your "authentic self" do you want to bring to work? How much of your "whole self" do you want to bring to work?

This is a domain that I'm researching, and I think that there's a way to sort of be "boundedly authentic." You're not totally unfiltered, but enough so that people respect it, even if they're not happy with the honesty it entails. This can help avoid some of the tacit misunderstandings, where you did something and someone interpreted it in a certain way and no one ever talked about it again. I agree with Nancy's strategy of owning up and checking in, perhaps even when you feel just a kernel of something that might be wrong. A few times I've thought, "Hmm, I'm not sure if this person is upset with me, but I'm going to preemptively say, 'Hey, listen, I'm really sorry that I couldn't make it to this event that you invited me to. I really wanted to, but this is what happened, and I hope . . . '" I've done that so there wasn't any opportunity for that small kernel of dissatisfaction to turn into something more.

Adapted from "Work Friendships Are Mostly Amazing and Sometimes Messy," Women at Work *podcast season 4, episode 4, November 4, 2019.*

19

What to Do When You Become Your Friend's Boss

by Ben Laker, Charmi Patel, Ashish Malik,
and Pawan Budhwar

How many hours will you spend with your co-workers over the course of your lifetime? If your job is a typical 9-to-5, that means you'll spend around eight hours a day, five days a week, for roughly 40 years, with the various people you work with. That equates to almost 90,000 hours total. So, a very long time.

Understandably, it would make sense for some of these connections to blossom into something more personal, like friendships. And that's a good thing, because having friends at work has been proven to increase job satisfaction, performance, and even productivity.

But there is a flip side to this. Close friendships also have the potential to cause friction, especially for those of us who work in hierarchal environments. Once you are promoted into a leadership position, you will inevitably be required to make tough decisions and evaluate the people on your team fairly, whether or not those people are your friends. This presents a real challenge if you are a new manager transitioning from the role of "work friend" to the role of "boss." When one person in a friendship moves up, the dynamic changes from that of equals to one of meritocracy.

Navigating the boss-friend dynamic is even more difficult today than it was 15 years ago. Before the existence of iPhones and social media, people generally knew much less about each other's private lives and collaborated mostly during office hours, when colleagues were available in-person. Today, new technologies and social sharing have made us reachable around the clock. Social etiquette is vastly different: 32% of workers are friends with their boss on Facebook, 19% follow each other on Instagram, and 7% on Snapchat. Sixty-eight percent of workers have their boss's cell number; 60% have met their significant other at work; 24% have visited their manager's residence; and 34% have solicited advice from their manager on personal matters.

With the rise in work friendships—and everyone knowing perhaps a little *too* much about each other— our latest research sought to identify the most effective way to manage your relationship with friends at work when you become their boss. We surveyed 200 male and 200 female recently promoted, first-time managers across 17 countries between January and August 2020 and asked them the following questions (among others):

- How do you maintain relationships with colleagues you are friends with?

- What happened to your friendships when you were promoted?

- How have your friendships been affected since you started your new role?

- Which of your work friends are you connected to on social media? Which platforms?

- What has changed since taking up your new role?

- What do you miss about the times before you became a boss?

- How has your behavior changed since you were promoted?

- Do your friends influence your decision-making? If so, how?

- Who do you offload to in times of stress?

We found, rather worryingly, that more than 90% of these first-time managers have struggled to navigate the boundaries between being a boss and a friend, and more than 70% have lost friendships since becoming a manager. But this still didn't answer our question: How do you manage someone you used to be friends with, and do it well?

To explore this question further, we analyzed data from our survey responses and then conducted follow-up interviews. Our goal was to hear about these managers' experiences in more detail and validate our findings. Through their responses, we identified five ways you can find the right balance between being a boss and a friend in "the information age."

Acknowledge the power shift

Relationships are fluid, and the ones that last often involve open and clear communication. But for this to happen, the people involved must learn to renegotiate or re-discuss the parameters of their relationship as it changes over time. Interestingly, more than 80% of the first-time managers we surveyed did not address how their promotions changed the power dynamics with their former peers—and regretted waiting too long to do so. Many were not proactive about acknowledging the new meritocracy and assumed any awkwardness that existed between them and their friends would disappear over time. But they were wrong. Many of their friendships have suffered as a result.

Healthy relationships require a degree of honesty, often described as "radical candor"—the ability to address the problem at hand, even if the feedback is harsh (as long as it comes from a place of caring). If you are a new leader managing a friend, it's important to face the reality and acknowledge that your relationship has changed sooner rather than later. You can do this by taking time to speak candidly to your friend, explaining how you feel about your new dynamic and how you'd like to keep any awkwardness at bay. Denying your feelings of discomfort may cause you to come across as disingenuous. At the same time, you need to empathize with your friend's situation. You could say, "I'm a little uncomfortable, too, bringing this up, but I value our friendship, and I want to maintain the bond we have. Some parts of our relationship might change at work, and I think it's better we call them out now so we're on the same page."

Accept your new role

Your behavior as a new manager should be congruent with your new responsibilities. Many first-time managers in our study found this difficult to do and often fell back into "friend mode" with their closest colleagues, particularly those they were connected to on social media. This often occurred when they felt stressed or angry. Many resorted to gossiping carelessly about work challenges or sharing confidential information.

Once you are the boss, it's essential to be respectful and treat all your team members equally. Never gossip with your friend about colleagues. When you're a junior colleague chatting with peers, this kind of talk may be inevitable, and even make you feel closer. But as a leader, it's your job to fix friction between team members and find solutions—not to get caught up in the problems. If you set a bad example, you will lose credibility and trust. After all, who wants to be led by someone who spreads negativity and encourages drama?

When you need to vent, find a colleague you can confide in at your own level, such as another manager, or a mentor with whom you can share and offload. You must also take care to do so in a safe space and never in the public realm of social media. Additionally, you can solicit a neutral party, like a coach, who has zero ties to your organization and your network.

Be consistent and fair

Another part of accepting your new role is being consistent in how you treat everyone on your team. This means that you cannot have favorites—and if you do, don't show it. If your team members suspect partiality, they may grow to resent you or the person you favor, and other toxic behavior could ensue.

For example, if you're heading out for lunch, extend the invitation to your whole team, not just those on your team you're most friendly with. In doing so, you may even discover new work-based friendships: In fact, more than 50% of our respondents reported developing new bonds with colleagues through this practice.

Don't let emotions get in the way of tough decisions

Being the boss means you have to accept that not everyone will like you, and that's OK. At the end of the day, the brutal truth is you're required to make the tough decisions. That's why you're the boss. It's important for you to recognize that if you're friends with an employee, you may be blinded to their flaws or you may not be able to place personal feelings aside so easily when you need to. This is why you have to be extra cautious about not letting your friendships influence your decisions, including raises, assignments, and layoffs.

Let's take layoffs, for example. This is probably the hardest leadership decision you'll ever face, and you should accept that letting go of employees (or firing a bad employee) is an unavoidable part of your job. You can't hold someone to a different set of standards just because you are friends—that's nepotism.

One way to treat everyone fairly is to put in place evaluation systems, such as objectives and key results, and use them for everyone equally, so you're relying on objective, not subjective, data.

Manage how much you share on social media

We don't recommend friending or following coworkers on social media, regardless of the platform. Your friends may use it to flaunt their bond with you, making their colleagues (your direct reports) jealous. For this reason, 10% of our respondents unfollowed and unfriended colleagues (and friends) after they were promoted. Many told us that doing so helped instill clearer boundaries between them and reduced the likelihood of oversharing. Others did not, choosing instead to tighten their privacy settings, allowing them to maintain a personal network separate from their work network.

Whichever strategy you adopt, our research suggests that, outside of work, you should never share any information with your work friends that wouldn't be shared inside the office. In doing so, you could damage credibility and undermine all of the preceding tips.

. . .

So remember—while workplace friendships have their benefits, they do have the potential to cause problems as your career paths diverge. Don't ignore the tough conversations. It's best to face the problem head-on as you transition from "work friend" to "boss."

Adapted from content posted on hbr.org, September 24, 2020.

20

When a Work Friendship Becomes Emotionally Draining

by Amy Gallo

Having a close friend at work can make you happier, more productive, and less likely to quit. But office friendships can have downsides, too. What should you do if you've gotten too emotionally involved? How do you make sure that your relationship doesn't impinge on your ability to get your job done? What sort of psychological boundaries should you put up? And how do you establish them in a way that doesn't hurt your colleague's feelings?

What the Experts Say

Empathy is an important component of emotional intelligence and thus an asset in the workplace; it helps you connect with others in a meaningful way. But you don't want to "let your emotions take over" and become so involved in a work friendship that it depletes your energy and productivity, says Susan David, author of *Emotional Agility*. Annie McKee, a senior fellow at the University of Pennsylvania Graduate School of Education and the author of *How to Be Happy at Work*, agrees. "It feels good to be needed but it can become a burden," she says. "It goes way beyond empathy if you're spending too much time helping someone figure out their problems or you get upset, worried, or maybe even scared about getting it right." If you feel like you and your coworker have gotten in too deep, here's what to do.

Watch for the signs

When you're neglecting your work to tend to an office friend, it's a sign that something needs to change. Other red flags include feeling like "you're on an emotional roller coaster" or like "you're more attached to the other person and their experiences than your own," McKee says. To assess whether your relationship is a healthy one, ask yourself a few questions: Is the relationship bringing me closer to the growth I want in my career? Are we both putting in the same amount of effort? Do I feel comfortable expressing thoughts and feelings that differ from my friend's? Can I see multiple sides to the problem the person is experiencing or just their own perspective?

Unfortunately, says David, "there's no clear line in the sand of what's OK and what's not." But if you answer no to any of these questions, consider making changes.

Don't blame the other person

If you conclude that the friendship isn't serving you, it's normal to get angry or annoyed. "There's an instinct to blame the other person and think, 'You drove me to this.' But that's a disempowering position to take," says David. Instead, think about your own role in creating the unhealthy dynamic. McKee suggests reflecting on what initially drew you to the person. Was it their personality? A work challenge you faced together? A hobby you share? This will give you useful information on how to disentangle your current relationship and will help you avoid similar situations in the future.

Don't cut them off entirely

In most cases, there's no need to abruptly end the relationship. You don't want to go "from being their best friend to refusing to having lunch with them because you're at the end of your rope," David says. "You might be shutting down an important connection." McKee agrees: "People think to change an unhealthy dynamic, you need to break it. But you don't have to. Slight shifts can actually move the relationship in the right direction without making anyone feel bad."

Change the tone of the conversation

It's tough to tell a friend that you want to spend less time with them. "Sometimes the relationship is healthy enough for you to be that direct, but it's rare," says McKee. "If they're self-aware and capable of having a deeply reflective conversation, you can dip your toe in the water and attempt to have the conversation." But in most scenarios, your strategy should be to "gradually shift" the way you speak with your friend. For example, "try to pick communication channels that are leaner," McKee says. "If you're spending a lot of time together in person, replace those interactions with phone calls. If you're spending more time on video or phone, replace that with a couple of emails." You want to create some physical distance and "tone down the intensity" of your interactions," says David. Whenever possible, "reemphasize your professional relationship" and talk about the importance of work.

Narrow the scope of your interactions

Decide where you want to draw the line. "Think about the problems your colleague shares with you and carve out one or two of them that you want to continue to help with," says McKee. Then "enable [the person] to take action" on the others. "Connect them with someone who can help," David says. She suggests saying something along the lines of, "I feel like we've been going in circles on this. You may benefit from seeing a coach."

Hold strong

It will take time to find a new balance. Your friend might not let you go willingly. But don't get sucked back in just because they push. If they ask you why you're not available for lunch, McKee suggests saying something along the lines of: "I miss our conversations too. But you know what I'm up against at work. I've really got to focus." Or use the opportunity to direct the person to the topic you want to discuss by saying, "Why don't we get together and talk about X?" If they make it hard, remind yourself that the short-term unpleasantness of drawing boundaries is less costly than the long-term drain on your energy.

Principles to Remember

DO:

- Watch out for signs that you're putting too much time or energy into your friendship and that it's hurting your productivity or performance

- Shift how you interact so that you're spending less time communicating with the person

- Offer to connect them with someone who can help them with their problems

DON'T:

- Place the blame on the other person; chances are you had a role in creating the unhealthy dynamic

- Cut them off entirely—that's often not feasible or pleasant

- Give in if they try to pull you back in; you need to hold strong to the boundaries you've set

Case Study 1: Encourage Your Colleague to Reach Out to Other People

Aliyah was on a team with her colleague Carlos for just over two years when the large accounting firm they worked for went through a merger. "As you can imagine, the whole thing was disruptive to everyone's life," Aliyah says.

Carlos regularly griped to her about the extra work that had been created. And Aliyah empathized with him. "I definitely got in on the complaining," she says. But once he realized that Aliyah was a sympathetic ear, he complained to her about other issues as well. He was moving apartments and then his sister was sick. "He had a lot going on," she says. "But it got off-kilter."

The amount of time they spent discussing his personal life was "way too high," Aliyah says, and their "work wasn't getting done." She knew she had to pull back. But just as she was mustering the courage to do so, Carlos was involved in a car accident that kept him out of work for several weeks. Aliyah found herself worrying about how much help he would need from her as a result. "I already felt like he had overdrawn on his bank account of how much I was willing to listen to him, but my natural human empathy required me to be there for him," she explains.

When another colleague pulled Aliyah aside to tell her that she was "really concerned" about how much time she was spending on the phone with Carlos and suggested she set some limits on her generosity, she knew it was time to make a change.

So she asked herself, "How do we dial it back?" The next time Carlos called, she encouraged him to reach out to a nonwork friend and talk to his parents. "With his consent, I [also] spoke to his manager about him needing to take some time off," which shifted some of the responsibility from her to the organization.

To Aliyah's surprise, Carlos didn't push back. "It definitely helped to have him reaching out to other people." When he eventually returned to the office, she also set new boundaries. She stopped picking up her phone every time he called and started sending email responses to his voicemails. If he stopped by her desk, she'd tell him she was busy trying to get work done and ask him to email her.

"I realized that his oversharing was about trying to make sure I was on his side, so now I just make sure he knows I am," she says. "It's a much more balanced relationship now. I think of him as stronger and he knows he can trust me."

Case Study 2: Use the Direct Approach If You Think It'll Work

Sophia Bland, the chief information officer of ResumeGo, a small business that offers career coaching and résumé-writing services, managed a close friend who she had known since college. Let's call her Carol.

"I had to juggle our professional relationship and our friendship on a regular basis," Sophia says. Sometimes this made it hard for Sophia to be objective. "There were instances where I let things slide for her that I didn't let slide for the other employees that I managed." For example, on a few occasions, she covered for Carol being late to work, delaying a morning group meeting without telling the rest of the team why.

In Sophia's view, Carol would take advantage of this "special treatment" and offer excuses for missed deadlines. "She'd tell me that she had such-and-such thing come up at home, or that she was having relationship issues with her boyfriend. I gave in to the excuses at first."

But over time, Sophia saw that Carol's behavior was affecting her coworkers. "This was when I knew I had to put an end to the nonsense." Still, she wasn't sure how to handle it. "I had to find a way to convey to her that she had to get her act together, while at the same time keeping our friendship intact."

Sophia decided to take Carol out to dinner. "This gave me the opportunity to sit her down and really talk face-to-face about the issues." She didn't level accusations, but she was direct. "I told her I empathized with the problems she was having in her life, but [explained] that it was unfair to [expect] the other team members to show up early and work harder because she'd been dropping the ball."

It was a civil conversation, and Carol seemed to get the message because she changed her behavior. The two women worked together for several more months before Carol found another job. "We're still friends," Sophia says. "Even though we no longer work together, we still see each other often and are on good terms."

Adapted from "What to Do When a Work Friendship Becomes Emotionally Draining" on hbr.org, January 21, 2019 (product #H04R8R).

21

Stay Friends with Your Work BFF—Even After One of You Leaves

by Shasta Nelson

I t can be painful when work friendships end not because they blow up or become disappointing but because of something far more innocent: One friend leaves the job.

While we may know on an intellectual level that the workplace won't feel the same when our friend leaves, we usually believe the relationship will continue outside of work. It's not until a few weeks or months later, when we no longer feel close to them, that we're likely to feel hurt, take the silence personally, and assume the friendship didn't mean as much to the other as we hoped it did.

That pain runs deep. So deep, in fact, that 30% of respondents in my 2019 *Friendships in the Workplace Survey* said their greatest fear about making friends at work was that it hurts too much to lose a friendship after the job ends. In fact, this is the fifth-highest-ranked fear about friendship at work—fear of losing the friendship *after* the job ranks even higher than the fear of losing that friendship *during* the job over a fight or breakup.

The news isn't all bad, though. While I have heard hundreds of stories about people feeling surprised and hurt by friendships that didn't survive outside the workplace, in that same survey, more than 61% of respondents claimed to still be close to a best friend from a previous job.

As I've written about previously, my research has shown that three relationship requirements drive how close we feel to others:

- **Consistency:** the shared experiences and regular interactions we have with each other

- **Vulnerability:** feeling like we know each other and can share who we are honestly

- **Positivity:** feeling rewarded by our relationship because we enjoy each other and feel accepted and appreciated

When a friend leaves our workplace, our relationship comes to a screeching halt simply because our consistency depended on us being paid to show up in the same space and spend time together. Without regular interaction (a lack of consistency), we'll soon feel like we don't know what's going on in each other's lives (a lack of vulnerability), and we'll stop feeling appreciated and having fun together (a lack of positivity).

The key to maintaining your relationship with a former coworker is figuring out what consistency looks like in the next chapter of your friendship. The following steps can help you reconnect with a friend you used to work with— or prevent you from drifting apart in the first place.

Initiate connection

When a friendship primarily lives in your "work-life container," the only way it can survive when one person no longer comes to that container is to create a new one. You have to figure out your new pattern, new habits, and new ways of staying connected. Unfortunately, none of that *just happens*—you have to make it happen.

You can do that before they leave the job by starting the conversation with something like, "I want to stay connected with you even in your new job! Any ideas how we can best go about seeing each other regularly now that we won't get to hang out all day?" Or if they've already left, you can reach out with an, "I miss you! Let's get together before too much more time passes. When works best for you?"

Then initiate again

Whether you're the one leaving or staying, recognize that it's going to take some serious effort to rebuild the scaffolding of your friendship outside of work. A relationship doesn't require that both people take turns initiating; it only requires that both people spend time together in a positive and meaningful way. For too long, we've equated initiating with caring more, so we're more prone to get our feelings hurt if we feel like we're the only one reaching out. The more important question is: Do we both enjoy spending time together, no matter whose idea it was?

The easiest approach is to set a standing date, like meeting for lunch every Monday, grabbing drinks over Zoom on the last Friday of every month, or calling each other for 15 minutes every day. This establishes a consistent pattern without requiring someone to reach out every time.

Or you might get in the habit of taking a few minutes to set your next date at the end of every get-together or call. You could also simply follow up after a conversation with a text or email saying, "As always, so good to connect with you. Do any of these dates work for you for us to do a repeat?"

Broaden the conversation

It may be tempting to focus conversations on updates from the old workplace, but if this friendship is going to thrive, it needs to be based on more than just the job you had in common. Plus, it's important to be mindful and compassionate of the circumstances of a friend leaving— they may feel left out or pushed out, or you may feel stuck or left behind. The goal is for both parties to feel safe sharing what's most important to them. You can foster that sense of safety by showing curiosity about your friend's new situation. One of my favorite questions to shape a conversation is, "I thought it would be fun to each share one thing we're loving about life right now and one thing that's causing stress." This allows each person to pick what they want to talk about most and ensures both people celebrate and support each other.

It can be hard to start a new pattern with someone and find the time to connect on top of everything else you're doing. But this moment is where you build on the strong foundation you already have. As you create new ways of spending time together and talking about new subjects, you transform a work best friend into a close friend and carry the peace that comes from knowing your friendship can survive life changes.

Adapted from content posted on hbr.org, November 11, 2020 (product #H05ZCM).

NOTES

Chapter 2

1. Amy C. Edmondson, *The Fearless Organization: Creating Psychological Safety in the Workplace for Learning, Innovation, and Growth* (Hoboken, NJ: John Wiley & Sons, 2018).

Chapter 4

1. Michael L. Slepian and Drew S. Jacoby-Senghor, "Identity Threats in Everyday Life: Distinguishing Belonging from Inclusion," *Social Psychological and Personality Science* 12, no. 3 (2021): 392–406.

2. Slepian and Jacoby-Senghor, "Identity Threats in Everyday Life."

Chapter 7

1. Ko Kuwabara, Claudius A. Hildebrand, and Xi Zou, "Lay Theories of Networking: How Laypeople's Beliefs About Networks Affect Their Attitudes Toward and Engagement in Instrumental Networking," *Academy of Management Review* 43, no. 1 (2016), doi: 10.5465/amr.2015.0076.

2. Tiziana Casciaro, Francesca Gino, and Miryam Kouchaki, "The Contaminating Effects of Building Instrumental Ties: How Networking Can Make Us Feel Dirty," *Administrative Science Quarterly* 59, no. 4 (2014): 705–735.

Notes

3. Herminia Ibarra, *Act Like a Leader, Think Like a Leader* (Boston: Harvard Business Review Press, 2015).

4. Mark S. Granovetter, "The Strength of Weak Ties," *American Journal of Sociology* 78, no. 6 (1973): 1360–1380.

Chapter 8

1. Costas Cavounidis and Kevin Lang, "Discrimination and Worker Evaluation," NBER Working Paper 21612, October 2015.

2. "Eighty-percent of professionals consider networking important to career success," LinkedIn Corporate Communications, June 22, 2017, https://news.linkedin.com/2017/6/eighty-percent-of -professionals-consider-networking-important-to-career-success.

3. Shelton Goode and Isaac Dixon, "Are Employee Resource Groups Good for Business? Two Experts Debate the Issue," shrm.org, August 25, 2016, https://www.shrm.org/hr-today/news/hr-magazine /0916/pages/are-employee-resource-groups-good-for-business.aspx.

Chapter 9

1. Julianne Holt-Lunstad et al., "Loneliness and Social Isolation as Risk Factors for Mortality: A Meta-Analytic Review," *Perspectives on Psychological Science* 10, no. 2 (2015): 227–237, doi: 10.1177 /1745691614568352.

Chapter 13

1. Coqual, *The Sponsor Dividend*, 2019, https://coqual.org/reports /the-sponsor-dividend/.

Chapter 15

1. David R. Hekman, Stefanie K. Johnson, Maw-Der Foo, and Wei Yang, "Does Diversity-Valuing Behavior Result in Diminished Performance Ratings for Non-White and Female Leaders?" *Academy of Management Journal* 60, no. 2 (2017): 771–797.

2. Belle Derks, Colette Van Laar, and Naomi Ellemers, "The Queen Bee Phenomenon: Why Women Leaders Distance Themselves from Junior Women," *Leadership Quarterly* 27, no. 3 (2016): 456–469.

3. McKinsey and Company, *Women in the Workplace 2016*, https://womenintheworkplace.com/2016#!.

Chapter 17

1. Working Mother Media, *The Gender Gap at the Top*, 2019, https://www.workingmother.com/sites/workingmother.com/files /attachments/2019/06/women_at_the_top_correct_size.pdf.

2. Center for Talent Innovation, *The Sponsor Dividend*, 2019, https:// www.talentinnovation.org/_private/assets/TheSponsorDividend _KeyFindingsCombined-CTI.pdf.

3. Lean In, "Working Relationships in the #MeToo Era," 2019, https://leanin.org/sexual-harassment-backlash-survey-results#!; Gillian Tan and Katia Porzecanski, "Wall Street Rule for the #MeToo Era: Avoid Women at All Cost," *Bloomberg*, December 3, 2018, https://www .bloomberg.com/news/articles/2018-12-03/a-wall-street-rule-for-the -metoo-era-avoid-women-at-all-cost.

4. McKinsey and Company, "Women in the Workplace 2016," September 2016, https://www.mckinsey.com/~/media/McKinsey /Business%20Functions/Organization/Our%20Insights/Women%20 in%20the%20Workplace%202016/Women-in-the-Workplace-2016.ashx; Shelley J. Correll and Caroline Simard, "Research: Vague Feedback Is Holding Women Back," hbr.org, April 29, 2016, https://hbr.org/2016/04 /research-vague-feedback-is-holding-women-back?autocomplete=true.

INDEX

Discussion Guide

Since the *Women at Work* podcast first launched, we've heard from all over the world that it has inspired discussions and listening groups. We hope that this book does the same—that you'll want to share what you've learned with others. The questions in this discussion guide will help you talk about the challenges women face in the workplace and how we can work together to overcome them.

You don't need to have read the book from start to finish to participate. To get the most out of your discussion, think about the size of your group. A big group has the advantage of spreading ideas more widely—whether throughout your organization or among your friends and peers—but might lose some of the honesty and connection a small group would have. You may want to assign someone to lead the discussion to ensure that all participants are included, especially if some attendees are joining virtually. And it's a good idea to establish ground rules around privacy and confidentiality. *Women at Work* topics touch on difficult issues surrounding sexism and racism, so consider using trigger warnings.

Finally, think about what you want to accomplish in your discussion. Do you want to create a network of mutual support? Hope to disrupt the status quo? Or are you simply looking for an empathetic ear? With your goals in mind, use the questions that follow to advance the conversation about women at work.

1. Tina Opie and Beth Livingston explain how shared sisterhood requires having the trust to tell one another how we really feel—that we can't empower one another if we can't show our true emotions to one another. Are you emotionally vulnerable at work, or are you more guarded? Which emotions are you comfortable showing? What aspects of yourself are you likely to hide, and why? What can we do to support our colleagues in opening up and being vulnerable?

2. Which of the three elements of trust discussed in chapter 3—positive relationships, good judgment/expertise, and consistency—affects how much you trust your colleagues? Do leaders in your organization, or a company where you have previously worked, show these characteristics? Which do you think you need to work on?

3. Do you think your organization acknowledges and understands the difference between diversity, inclusion, and belonging—and fosters all three? Where do you think improvements could and should be made?

4. Inga Carboni says that women often feel inauthentic, manipulative, or selfish when they are networking.

How do you feel when you are networking? What do you attribute these feelings to? Has the way you feel about networking shifted over time, and what do you think brought about those changes?

5. What are the strengths and weaknesses of your network? What types of connections are over- or underrepresented? Where do you want to make improvements, and how might achieving more gender balance in your network help your career?

6. How has remote work changed your approach to networking? What aspects of connecting are easier in a remote setting, and which aspects are more difficult?

7. Rebecca Knight recommends steps for making sure your network is composed of real and beneficial connections: actively *deciding* who you want to stay in touch with, acknowledging that you can't stay in touch with everyone, and auditing your contacts from time to time. Have you ever taken steps like these, and what effects did they have on your network?

8. Have you ever been in a sponsorship relationship before, either as a sponsor or a protégé? In that relationship, was there ever a formal "ask" or "offer" of sponsorship between you? What did that look like?

9. The title of chapter 15 says it all: "Don't Underestimate the Power of Women Supporting Each Other at Work."

Are the professional relationships between women at your organization generally more supportive or competitive? Have you seen extraordinary outcomes from women supporting other women—or *not* supporting other women?

10. What is the dynamic between men and woman at your organization? Are they allies to women and encourage their growth? Do you think the widespread awareness and outrage around sexual harassment in the workplace after the #MeToo movement has led to more or fewer sponsorship opportunities between male sponsors and female protégés?

11. Has your ability to do your job well ever been impeded by work friendships? Have you ever been put in an uncomfortable position by supporting a work friend?

12. Have you ever been able to restore a ruptured relationship at work? What did that look like? How long did it take for trust to be fully regained?

13. Have you ever become your friend's boss (or vice versa)? Were you able to retain your friendship? In what ways did it change? Did either of you face the transition "head-on," as the authors of chapter 19 suggest?

14. Do you maintain your relationships with work friends after you or they have left your organization? Have you

been able to establish new rhythms of communication and broaden your conversation beyond work? What has that looked like?

15. Overall, how has this book changed your thinking about making real connections at work? Do you see trust, networking, sponsorship, and work friendships in a different light now?

ABOUT THE CONTRIBUTORS

Amy Bernstein, *Women at Work* cohost, is the editor of *Harvard Business Review* and vice president and executive editorial director of Harvard Business Publishing. Follow her on Twitter @asbernstein2185.

Emily Caulfield, *Women at Work* cohost, is a senior designer at *Harvard Business Review.*

Amy Gallo, *Women at Work* cohost, is a contributing editor at *Harvard Business Review* and the author of the *HBR Guide to Dealing with Conflict* (Harvard Business Review Press, 2017) and *Getting Along: How to Work with Anyone (Even Difficult People)* (Harvard Business Review Press, 2022). She writes and speaks about workplace dynamics. Watch her TEDx talk on conflict and follow her on Twitter @amyegallo.

Nicole Torres, *Women at Work* cohost (seasons 1–4), is an editor at Bloomberg Opinion based in London and a former senior editor at *Harvard Business Review.*

Shawn Achor is the *New York Times*–bestselling author of *Big Potential*, *The Happiness Advantage*, and *Before Happiness*. He serves as the chief experience officer for BetterUp. His TED talk is one of the most popular, with over 11 million views. He has lectured or researched at over a third of the *Fortune* 100 companies and in 50 countries, as well as for the NFL, Pentagon, and White House. He is leading a series of courses on "21 Days to Inspire Positive Change" with the Oprah Winfrey Network.

Rania H. Anderson is an international keynote speaker, author, and executive business coach who transforms the way men and women work together. She is the author of *WE: Men, Women, and the Decisive Formula for Winning at Work* and *Undeterred*.

Pawan Budhwar is a professor of international human resource management at Aston Business School at Aston University.

Inga Carboni is a professor at the College of William & Mary's Mason School of Business and the author of *Connect the Dots*.

Rosalind Chow is an associate professor at Carnegie Mellon University's Tepper School of Business.

Dorie Clark is a marketing strategist and professional speaker who teaches at Duke University's Fuqua School of Business. She is the author of *Entrepreneurial You, Reinventing You*, and *Stand Out*.

Amy Edmondson is the Novartis Professor of Leadership and Management at Harvard Business School. She is the author of *The Fearless Organization*.

Joseph Folkman is the president of Zenger/Folkman, a leadership development consultancy. He is a coauthor of the HBR article "Making Yourself Indispensable" and the book *Speed*. Follow him on Twitter @joefolkman.

Sylvia Ann Hewlett is an economist, the CEO of Hewlett Consulting Partners, and the founder and chair emeritus of Coqual, formerly the Center for Talent Innovation. She is the author of 14 books, including *Off-Ramps and On-Ramps*; *Forget a Mentor, Find a Sponsor*; *Executive Presence*; and *The Sponsor Effect*.

Herminia Ibarra is the Charles Handy Professor of Organizational Behavior at London Business School. Prior to joining LBS, she served on the INSEAD and Harvard Business School faculties. She is the author of *Act Like a Leader, Think Like a Leader* and *Working Identity* (both Harvard Business Review Press, 2015 and 2003, respectively). Follow her on Twitter @HerminiaIbarra.

Pooja Jain-Link is executive vice president at Coqual, where she coleads the organization's research and advisory services practices that examine workplace culture and the systemic change needed to create equity. She's led research for many Coqual studies, including *Being Black in Corporate America, The Sponsor Dividend,* and *Wonder Women in STEM and Companies That Champion Them.*

Julia Taylor Kennedy is executive vice president at Coqual, where she coleads the organization's research and leadership development practices to support diverse, inclusive, and equitable leadership in the workplace. She's led research for many Coqual studies, including *Being Black in Corporate America, The Power of Belonging,* and *The Sponsor Dividend.*

Rebecca Knight is a senior correspondent at *Insider,* covering careers and the workplace. Previously she was a freelance journalist and a lecturer at Wesleyan University. Her work has been published in the *New York Times, USA Today,* and the *Financial Times.*

Ben Laker is a professor of leadership at Henley Business School, University of Reading.

Beth Livingston is an assistant professor of management and organizations at the University of Iowa Tippie College of Business. Her research interests lie primarily in gender, discrimination, and work-family, with additional interests in diversity and stereotypes.

Ashish Malik is an associate professor of strategic human resources management at Newcastle Business School at the University of Newcastle, Australia. Follow him on Twitter @maliknewcas.

Anthony J. Mayo is the Thomas S. Murphy Senior Lecturer of Business Administration in the Organizational Behavior unit of Harvard Business School.

Anne Welsh McNulty has invested in elevating entrepreneurial leaders and nurturing promising students for over 25 years as cofounder and president of the McNulty Foundation. A trailblazer for women in finance, she was a managing director of Goldman Sachs and a senior executive of the Goldman Sachs Hedge Fund Strategies Group.

Mark Mortensen is an associate professor of organizational behaviour at INSEAD. He researches, teaches, and consults on issues of collaboration, organizational design, and new ways of working, and leadership.

Shasta Nelson is a friendship expert and a leading voice on loneliness and creating healthy relationships. Her research is found in her three books, including *The*

Business of Friendship on why we need to foster better relationships in our jobs. Her interviews have been featured on TEDx, the *New York Times*, *HBR Ideacast*, and *The Steve Harvey Show*. For more information, visit www. TheBusinessofFriendship.com.

Tina Opie is the founder of Opie Consulting Group LLC, where she advises large firms in the financial services, entertainment, media, beauty, educational, and healthcare industries. She is an award-winning researcher, consultant, Associate Professor of Management at Babson College, and Visiting Scholar at Harvard Business School. Her work has appeared in such outlets as *O Magazine*, the *Washington Post*, the *Boston Globe*, and *Harvard Business Review*. She is also a regular commentator on HBR's *Women at Work* podcast and Greater Boston's NPR affiliate television station WGBH.

Charmi Patel is an associate professor in International Human Resource Management at Henley Business School.

Julianna Pillemer is an assistant professor of management and organizations at New York University's Stern School of Business. Her research examines the complex dynamics of interpersonal connections at work.

Laura Morgan Roberts is a professor of practice at the University of Virginia's Darden School of Business and the coeditor of *Race, Work, and Leadership: New Perspectives on the Black Experience* (Harvard Business Review Press, 2019).

Nancy P. Rothbard is the David Pottruck Professor of Management at the Wharton School, University of Pennsylvania.

Michael Slepian is the Sanford C. Bernstein & Co. Associate Professor of Leadership and Ethics at Columbia Business School. Follow him on Twitter @michaelslepian.

David G. Smith is an associate professor in the Johns Hopkins Carey Business School. He is the coauthor, with W. Brad Johnson, of *Good Guys: How Men Can Be Better Allies for Women in the Workplace* and *Athena Rising: How and Why Men Should Mentor Women* (both Harvard Business Review Press, 2020 and 2019, respectively).

Jack Zenger is the CEO of Zenger/Folkman, a leadership development consultancy. He is a coauthor the HBR article "Making Yourself Indispensable" and the book *Speed: How Leaders Accelerate Successful Execution.* Follow him on Twitter @jhzenger.

ABOUT THE PODCAST

Women face gender discrimination throughout our careers. It doesn't have to derail our ambitions—but how do we prepare to deal with it? There's no workplace orientation session about narrowing the wage gap, standing up to interrupting male colleagues, or taking on many other issues we encounter at work. So HBR staffers Amy Bernstein, Amy Gallo, and Emily Caulfield are untangling some of the knottiest problems. They interview experts on gender, tell stories about their own experiences, and give lots of practical advice to help you succeed in spite of the obstacles.

Listen and subscribe:

Apple Podcasts, Google Podcasts, Spotify, RSS

Inspiring conversations, advancing together

Based on the HBR podcast of the same name, **HBR's Women at Work series** spotlights the real challenges and opportunities women face throughout their careers—and provides inspiration and advice on today's most important workplace topics.

Engage with HBR content the way you want, on any device.

With HBR's new subscription plans, you can access world-renowned **case studies** from Harvard Business School and receive **four free eBooks**. Download and customize prebuilt **slide decks and graphics** from our **Visual Library**. With HBR's archive, top 50 best-selling articles, and five new articles every day, HBR is more than just a magazine.

Subscribe Today
hbr.org/success